Finding Love

Finding Love

An Appreciative Inquiry into Christian Talk about Sin and Salvation

ANDREW LESLIE CALLANDER

Foreword by Murray Rae

WIPF & STOCK · Eugene, Oregon

FINDING LOVE

An Appreciative Inquiry into Christian Talk about Sin and Salvation

Copyright © 2021 Andrew Leslie Callander. All rights reserved. Except for brief quotations in critical publications or reviews, no part of this book may be reproduced in any manner without prior written permission from the publisher. Write: Permissions, Wipf and Stock Publishers, 199 W. 8th Ave., Suite 3, Eugene, OR 97401.

Wipf & Stock
An Imprint of Wipf and Stock Publishers
199 W. 8th Ave., Suite 3
Eugene, OR 97401

www.wipfandstock.com

PAPERBACK ISBN: 978-1-7252-9323-6
HARDCOVER ISBN: 978-1-7252-9324-3
EBOOK ISBN: 978-1-7252-9326-7

02/15/21

Dedicated to the memory of Thora Louise Callander (1922–2001)

Contents

Foreword by Murray Rae | ix
Acknowledgments | xi
Introduction | xiii

1 **God Is Love**—so what does that make us? | 1
2 **Faith**—so whose faith saves who? | 12
3 **Sinners**—so who are we speaking to? | 21
4 **Sin**—so what are we talking about? | 29
5 **Christ Died for Our Sins**—so what has God done and for whom? | 39
6 **God's Perfect World**—so what went wrong? | 52
7 **God's Good Creation**—so did anything go right? | 63
8 **Repentance**—so who needs to do it? | 74
9 **I Am the Man**—so what is God doing about it? | 82
10 **The Righteousness of God**—so is this a good thing or a bad thing? | 92
11 **The Salvation of God**—so what does a saved person look like? | 105
   Finding Love | 119

Bibliography | 123

Foreword

THE CHRISTIAN CHURCH IS called to be, among other things, the bearer of good news. It is called to proclaim the news that God, who is the creator of all things and who will bring them to completion at the last, has come among us in the person of his beloved Son in order to gather the world once more into the embrace of his love. The Gospel of John puts the matter clearly and succinctly: it is because "God so loved the world that he sent his only Son" (John 3:16). This drama of divine love is worked out through the whole course of Jesus' life. It is presented again and again in Jesus' teaching, in the parable of a lost sheep gathered once more into the shepherd's arms, in the story of a wayward son whose return home is greeted with tears of joy and an extravagant display of parental love, in the declaration that Jesus has come to seek and to save the lost. This same divine love is seen in Jesus' engagement with those who were despised, in the company he keeps with outcasts and sinners, and in the forgiveness and the healing touch he offers again and again to those who were broken and diseased. This drama of divine love reaches its climax, of course, in Jesus' own death and resurrection; it is seen in his readiness to take upon himself the very worst of human brutality, and in his dying prayer: "Father, forgive them, for they know not what they do." His resurrection from the dead then reveals that God's love and God's promise of abundant life is not defeated even when we do our worst.

This is the good news, that neither the world's destiny nor our identity as human beings are determined by our human weakness or by our defiance of God. Our identity and the ultimate telos of creation are determined rather by the steadfast love of God. They are determined in the end, as it was in the beginning, by the God who delights in all that he has made and whose love for every one of us gives us a dignity and a worth that cannot ever be lost. This is the good news. Why then is the church so often perceived as the bearer of bad news? Why is the message the church delivers to the world so often heard as a message of judgment and condemnation? Why are "Christian" voices on social media, to take one of the most problematic arenas of human discourse, so often filled with hatred and so ready to condemn?

In this book, Andrew Callander addresses frankly the sad situation of a church that appears too often to have lost sight of the good news and that presents instead a message which renders inaudible the gospel it is called to proclaim. The point of Andrew's writing, however, is not to condemn the church, but to help it to see once more the goodness of the news with which it has been entrusted, the news that God so loves the world that he sent his only Son. There is to be sure a call that follows this evangelical declaration, a call to belief and to discipleship, and indeed to repentance. But these acts of faith, enabled by the Spirit, are presented again and again in Scripture, not as a fearful response to a gospel of condemnation, but as the joyous acknowledgment of the God who has created and sustained us, and who loves us with the same extravagant giving of himself that Jesus portrays in the father of the always-beloved prodigal son.

Proclamation of the good news in the way proposed in this book does not mean, as some seem to fear, that human sin is no longer to be taken seriously, or that the wrath of God is to be excised from the church's proclamation. These features of the biblical account of our human situation are part of the truth of things and are not to be done away with, but they can only be spoken of truthfully when set in the context of divine love. Abstracted from that context, the church's talk of sin and wrath have nothing to do anymore with the God made known to us in Jesus. Such talk is merely a clashing cymbal. It produces the discordant tones that serve only to drive people away from the truly good news that Scripture declares.

This book is an attempt to listen carefully to Scripture, to listen above all to Scripture's declaration that God is love, and to read all else in the light of that declaration. That is the proper thing to do if we are to understand Scripture aright. This book is written with a pastor's heart. Andrew has seen the damage done when the gospel is misconstrued; he has seen the costliness of a gospel falsely proclaimed. His aim, as stated in the opening pages, is to help us express the truth of the gospel in ways that better reflect the loving heart of God. Surely then, it will be the message that the world needs to hear.

Murray Rae
Professor of Theology
University of Otago

Acknowledgments

I WISH TO THANK the people of St James' Church New Plymouth who have resourced me as their minister to wrestle with Holy Scripture and what faith in Jesus means in our twenty-first-century context—and then allowed me to report back to them Sunday by Sunday on this great theme that compels us all.

I am deeply grateful to Murray Rae, under whose teaching I have been greatly enriched, for supervising this project and writing the foreword. Also Chelsea Putt, whose proofreading and encouragement have helped me more than she may ever know. I also thank Kevin Ward, Diane Gilliam-Weeks, and Sue Fenton for their willingness to write endorsements for this book.

To the small group I participated with when I first began to share my thinking in response to our reading Rob Voyle's *An Appreciative Inquiry Paradigm* together, who asked questions like, "How can we apply this to the gospel as a whole?" and made comments like, "What you have presented has been the highlight of the week," and especially, "You must write!" My deepest thanks.

And my family—for your love, encouragement, and support I am forever grateful.

Introduction

WHEN I WAS ABOUT fourteen my mother told me a tragic story. At the time I wasn't able to understand just how tragic it was. But as I have reflected on it as an adult, as a Christian, and especially now as a Christian *minister*—it fills me with great sadness. It also fills me with great anger. She told me that when she was a young woman she worked in a shop. One day a young man came in and she felt strongly that God wanted her to share the gospel with him. But my mother was timid—and so she didn't. As a result she experienced a deep sense of guilt thinking she had disobeyed God. She confided in a trusted Christian who suggested to her that she might have committed "the unforgivable sin." I am convinced this word of judgment blighted my mother's life to her dying day.

Consequently I have become highly sensitized to the way many well-meaning Christians use the language of the Bible in ways that I consider irresponsible and harmful—and therefore contrary to the true heart of God. This is especially true of the word "sin." As a result I have spent a lot of time thinking about the ways we Christians speak of faith in Jesus Christ: the theologies we express, the language we use, and the illustrations and metaphors we employ. While I am convinced that what Jesus has done and continues to do in the lives of people and in our world is profoundly true and significant, nevertheless I am deeply distressed by what much of institutionalized Christianity has done to him and in his name.

Moreover, I am convinced people instinctively know this. In many previously Christianized countries onetime believers have been leaving institutionalized Christianity in droves: sick of the narrow-mindedness, bigotry, and hypocrisy; repelled by the moral unbelievability of many of its doctrines; and disillusioned by (for want of a better term) the "far away from the true heart of Jesus-ness" that so often seems center stage of much Christian energy and activity. Quite understandably these people have become disenchanted with the institution, voted with their feet, and left. Yet not all these leavers have given up on Jesus—they have just become deeply sceptical of a certain *kind* of Christianity. As I once heard it somewhat cynically expressed, "For many people Jesus is still a trusted *brand*—it's just that they have lost confidence in the traditional *outlets*."

Therefore, I try to listen to this disillusioned and no-longer-Christian critique of Christianity—as well as to the frequently hostile critique from wider secular culture: namely, that this kind of Christianity is not only redundant but a negative influence in the world fostering intolerance, bigotry, racism, homophobia, violence, and a whole range of shame-based dysfunctions. I try to listen to this critique because I believe there is an instinctive knowledge of God in much of this. In the same way God used the pagan nations of the ancient past to bring his saving judgment to bear upon an errant Israel, I am convinced God is also using those who have left the institutional church and those living within contemporary secular culture to be instrumental in bringing God's saving judgment to bear upon an errant church. God is doing this—as God has always done—not in order to condemn the church, but in order that it may become again what it has always been called to be: a human witness in the world to the grace and truth of God as revealed in Jesus Christ. Therefore, I regard this critique as a welcome prophetic voice that we still-institutionalized Christians ignore at our peril.

A key resource that has helped bring my thoughts together for this book, and which has given me its title, is a short reading by Rob Voyle—"An Appreciative Inquiry Paradigm for Transitional Ministry."[1] What especially struck me is Voyle saying:

> Much of religion and psychology shares an interest in trying to determine what is wrong with humanity. . . . Religion gives us catalogues of sin, as in the book of Leviticus. . . . Yet [it] . . . provide[s] no equally robust classification of human joys or life-giving qualities.[2]

He goes on to argue that focusing on what is *wrong* with people locks them into unproductive cycles of guilt, shame, and failure; whereas focusing on what is life-giving orients them toward an open future in which they are empowered to reimagine and incarnate new ways of being and doing. The

---

1. Voyle, "Appreciative Inquiry," 122–45.
2. Voyle, "Appreciative Inquiry," 122.

more people focus on what is working in their lives (as opposed to what is wrong) and what is life-giving (as opposed to shame-inducing) the more these life-giving realities grow. In other words, the stories we tell ourselves and others about who we believe we and they are is a form of speech-act—words that have the power to bring into existence the things of which they speak and therefore words that have the power of creation or destruction and of life or death. However, Voyle says that focusing on shame

> rarely creates sustainable change. . . . When a person is continually shamed over a period of time, the shamed person will be motivated to destroy those who are shaming them.[3]

This is very strong language. I can well understand some or perhaps even many shamed people being motivated to want to destroy those who have shamed them. However, I think the shame response is more nuanced than this. As with most things, context is all important. I know from my own experience behaviors that I have been rebuked for by others (and therefore felt shame about) have, on reflection, concerned things that I now acknowledge I should not have been doing. When this rebuke has been delivered by someone who I know genuinely loves me and seeks the very best for me, the shame I have experienced has not motivated me to want to destroy them. Rather, this experience of shame (once I have recovered from my initial angry egotistical self-defensive responses) has prompted me to think better of myself and prompted a change of heart. Indeed we sometimes speak, as does the Bible, of people who fail to do this—people who are described as being shameless. That is, people who on account of their behavior (and the loving rebuke of others) ought to experience the psychological and emotional feelings of shame which ought to motivate them to think better of themselves and in this way modify their behavior—but who don't!

I consider these words of Voyle prophetic—that people seeking to destroy Christian influence in the world (or at least removing themselves from institutionalized Christianity) is a natural and expected response to an institution that for far too long *has* focused on what is wrong with people by addressing them as "sinners." In this way the gospel has often not been proclaimed within an overarching context of love that genuinely seeks the best for others (or at least has not been *heard* in this way) and therefore it has far too often sounded like a proclamation of Christian judgment and

---

3. Voyle, "Appreciative Inquiry," 128.

condemnation instead of what it truly is and ought to be—the proclamation of God's life-giving grace in Jesus Christ.

In seeking to recover this overarching context of love, Voyle has developed three fundamental assumptions that sit at the center of what he calls *The Appreciative Way*.

ASSUMPTION A: At the heart of the universe is love which is the source of our existence and our purpose for being.[4]

He argues that if our goal is to *find* or *secure* love—God's or anyone else's—then we will live in fear. This is because our minds will forever turn to the anxiety-inducing question concerning our adequacy for this task. Do we possess the resources or attractiveness or *good-enoughness* to merit and secure the love of another? Or if we succeed in finding love then our anxiety turns to how we can maintain what we have gained and all the things that may threaten our possession and cause us to lose it. However, Voyle argues, if our fundamental conviction is that we are "already enfolded in eternal loving-kindness,"[5] then this liberates us from the fear-inducing task of thinking that our life work consists of mounting a great search for love—and the anxiety of wondering if we are adequate for this task, worthy enough to win or deserve the love of another, and whether we can ever hold on to it if we do in fact find it.

ASSUMPTION B: The deepest longing of the human heart is for acceptance, and the only changes that will be sustainable are those that result in greater self-acceptance and acceptance from and for others.[6]

Voyle observes that,
> while acceptance is the deepest longing of the human heart, we often experience life as a state of alienation. We experience alienation from our self, our abilities, and our deepest potential; from our neighbor; and from God, the source of our existence.[7]

---

4. Voyle, "Appreciative Inquiry," 124.
5. Voyle, "Appreciative Inquiry," 125.
6. Voyle, "Appreciative Inquiry," 125.
7. Voyle, "Appreciative Inquiry," 125.

Nevertheless, following his own advice that the solution to the problem of alienation is not focusing on alienation (which is simply another dimension of focusing on what is wrong), Voyle says we must instead focus on *reconciliation* and *collaboration*. He explains that focusing on diagnosing and treating alienation

> is a sophisticated [method] of judgment and blame, and when used with social systems, regardless of intentions, it will be experienced as alienating. Some people within the system will always feel blamed and experience alienation, which will not incline their hearts toward life-giving outcomes.[8]

He emphasizes that in order to experience acceptance people need for their existence to be recognized and affirmed, their voice heard and their story listened to, their talents recognized and received as a unique contribution, and their dreams and hopes for a better tomorrow acknowledged and blessed—all by the community to which they look for acceptance.

ASSUMPTION C: At any given moment, people are doing the best they know how to in that context.[9]

This means that we must understand all human behavior (regardless of how seemingly dysfunctional and damaging it appears on the surface) is somehow bearing witness to a positive intention. Voyle emphasizes that very often the positive intent will lie hidden below the surface—perhaps many layers down—and that we must not confuse the behavior itself with the underlying positive intention. However, returning to his fundamental point, he reiterates that focusing on dysfunctional behavior without trying to discover the positive intent that lies behind it simply creates shame—and that focusing on shame seldom creates sustainable change.

However, before making use of Voyle's three assumptions in relation to my project I want to first express them in my own words. I do this in order to shape them in a way that gives greater focus to my specific interests and also to highlight the connections that are implicit thus creating a narrative.

> *Assumption A*: God, who is the source of our being and the goal of our existence, is love. This means that we have been created *in* love, *by* love, and *for* love, and this constitutes the whole purpose

---

8. Voyle, "Appreciative Inquiry," 126.
9. Voyle, "Appreciative Inquiry," 127.

of our being—to be awakened to the fact that we are already enfolded in God's eternal loving-kindness and to be consciously and experientially incorporated into this love.

Assumption B: Although this knowledge is often obscure to us, all that we are and do *somehow* bears witness to this God-created purpose for our human being. This means that our deepest human need and longing, and thus what constitutes our fundamental humanity, is being loved and loving in return—being accepted, valued, and affirmed. Conversely, our deepest human fear—and thus the greatest threat to our being truly human—is to exist in a state of lovelessness and thus believing ourselves to be alienated, rejected, and valueless.

Assumption C: Therefore—given both our knowledge and ignorance, our wholeness and brokenness, whether openly or secretly, with conscious awareness or merely by instinct—at any given moment we are doing the best we know to secure this love or else to guard ourselves against the hurts of failed love. So regardless of how our behavior manifests itself on the surface, the great inner driver behind all that we are and do is our quest to secure acceptance, value, and affirmation; and to avoid alienation, rejection, and shame. It is seeking these positives and avoiding these negatives in ways that miss the purpose of God that lies at the root of all our anxieties, dysfunctions, and miseries.

If these assumptions are true then we must acknowledge that God's love, by its very nature, is relational. This is because in order to love there must be both a giver and a receiver—both a lover and one who is loved. This being so, the essential category we must think of God in terms of is that God is a *relational* being and therefore at the core of the very being of God is *loving relationality*—the love of the triune God the Bible reveals to us as Father, Son, and Holy Spirit. If our essence and existence derives from the loving relationality of this triune God then the thing that most truly constitutes the essence of our humanity (and thus the way we most truly correspond to the being of God) is our being consciously incorporated into and participating in the love of God in genuinely relational and experiential ways. Furthermore, in order to accord with the purposes of God, this participation in God's love needs to flow outward to inform and transform all our other relationships as well—with ourselves, with others, and with the world. Being incorporated into the love of God and all that flows from this must therefore constitute our greatest joy. Conversely, our greatest misery must be to live in alienation from and in contradiction to God's love—and therefore in contradiction to our true selves, others as they truly are, and the world as it truly is.

What follows is me taking these thoughts from Voyle and using them to critically reflect on what I have observed in the contemporary Christian world—in particular the theologies that are typically expressed, the language used, and the illustrations and metaphors employed to speak of what God has done and is doing in and through Jesus Christ. And then to explore how we can express the truth of God in ways that better reflect the true heart of God.

1

God Is Love
—so what does that make us?

Twice in 1 John 4:7–21 we are told, "God is love." In making this profoundly important statement John is not simply telling us that God is *loving*—as if love is simply one of the many *attributes* God possesses alongside others. Much more than this, John wants us to understand that at the very heart and center of God's nature and being—the fundamental essence that constitutes the core of God's very God-ness—*is love*. This being so, God does not possess some other inner motivator that sits at a deeper, more elemental place within his being that might, on occasions, displace his love. What this means is that God's love has no reason beyond itself and therefore God does not use love as an instrumental technique to achieve some other purpose that isn't love. God's love is therefore genuine and so God respects the freedom and the integrity of those who are the relational objects and subjects of his love. Consequently God never manipulates or coerces those he loves into any way of being they do not freely choose. This is why God gives all his relationships time and space to develop and flourish. God, in both creating us and the world, intends and enables a history of encounter to take place that allows all the different dimensions of loving relationality to be experienced and to grow. God's love therefore creates room for development and change, joy and sorrow, alienation and reconciliation, sin and grace, judgment and salvation.

In John 17:24–26 we are given a glimpse into the inner life of God's triune loving relationality. Jesus prays on behalf of his disciples:

> Father... you loved me before the creation of the world.... I have made you known to them, and will continue to make you known, in order that the love you have for me may be in them and that I myself may be in them.[1]

Here Jesus reveals two amazing truths. First, he reveals the loving relationality of God. He speaks of the relationship of intimate love between Father and Son—"You loved me before the creation of world." Jesus reveals what was going on within the inner being of God before creation and therefore before there existed anything external to the being of God—that from all eternity God is and has always been a God of loving fellowship, communication, and self-giving grace. Second, he reveals that it is God's desire to welcome us into this same relationship of loving communion that Jesus enjoys with his Father—"that the love you have for me may be in them." Jesus reveals therefore that from all eternity it has always been God's desire and intention to invite and enable those he has created to participate in and enjoy God's love.

Now in speaking of these things it is so very important we guard against three kinds of *individualism* that are so prevalent within contemporary Western Christian culture. The first is individualism with respect to *personhood*—the idea that our personal identity is a self-created accomplishment independent of God or the wider community within which we live. The second is individualism with respect to *relationship*—the idea that Christian faith centers upon a personal and private relationship with God independent of others or the world. And the third is individualism with respect to *responsibility*—the idea that our relationship with God is something that we, by our individual faithfulness toward God, are primarily responsible for accomplishing and sustaining independent of the faithfulness of God (and others) toward us.[2]

One of the great myths of modern Western culture is that our personal identity is a self-created accomplishment—that it depends upon the vision of self we as individuals choose to create (or adopt) and the force of will we bring to the fulfillment of this vision. Now of course there is much truth in the idea that our identity is, to a significant degree, determined by

---

1. Unless otherwise stated, all Bible quotations are from the New International Version.

2. My thinking concerning these three individualisms has been deeply influenced by David Bentley Hart's meditation "What Is a Person? A Reflection on the Divine Image," 130–58, and Torrance, *Worship, Community & the Triune God of Grace*.

our individual choices. Nevertheless, a moment's thought enables us to see that so much of what we imagine our personal identity to consist of in fact comes from others. If the identical genetic biology that constitutes *me* had instead come into existence within a different set of circumstances—a different family, group of friends, educational philosophy, life circumstance, country, language, culture, political system, state of economic development, historical epoch—this would have given rise to a very different version of "me" than the one I currently am. What this means is that who we are, to a very significant degree, is formed in community with others. The truth is that we are deeply and indelibly shaped by an entire network of people, both past and present, who have produced the language and cultural environments within which we have been shaped; the visionaries who have created the literature, music, and artistic beauty that have inspired our spirits; the people of action who have forged the political, economic, and technological systems that have determined the kind of world we inhabit; and the philosophers, scientists, and spiritual teachers who have given rise to what we regard as "knowledge" and "truth" that has shaped the way we think, the convictions we hold, and the values we cherish. Indeed it is no exaggeration to say that, one way or another, this network of people through whom we are shaped actually constitutes *all humanity*. Each person who has ever lived (for better or for worse) has both influenced, and been influenced by, others. These in turn have influenced still others, and so on, in an unbroken chain of human connection from the dawn of creation down to the present moment of every "me" who has ever lived.

Recognizing this unbroken chain of human connection leads to the second myth of individualism that is so prevalent within contemporary Western Christian culture that we need to guard ourselves against. This, as already noted, is individualism with respect to *relationship*—the idea that Christian faith centers upon a personal and private relationship with God independent of others or the world. If it is true (as Christians typically profess) that God loves and cares deeply about us as individuals and seeks to enter into a personal relationship with us, then this must mean that God also cares deeply about all the people we care deeply about. We can easily understand this at a human level. If someone professes their deep love or abiding friendship for me, yet has no interest or concern for my family, friends, neighbors, customers, teammates, fellow students, work colleagues, those I share Communion with, and so on—if all they are interested in is a personal and private relationship with *me* as an individual that excludes those I am connected to, find my sense of identity with, and care deeply about; then I would rightly regard this "love" or "friendship" they profess to be sinister and self-serving. Likewise if I profess my love or friendship to someone *I* care deeply about, yet am uninterested in the people *they* are connected to and care about; then they would rightly question the kind of "love" and "friendship" *I* claim to profess. They would rightly ask, "Why would I want to be in relationship with anyone who doesn't care about the people I care about?" We have to ask therefore, "What sort of god would *God* be to profess his love for us *as individuals*, yet be uncaring concerning all the people we care deeply about—and so why would we want to be in relationship with such a god? Therefore, for God to genuinely care deeply for me as an individual—an individual who has been formed in relationship with others—then if God is a god of love he must also care deeply about all the people in my network of relationships who I care about. But for God to genuinely care deeply about all the people in *my* network of relationships, then God must also care deeply about all the people in *their* networks of relationships—and so on in an unbroken chain of human connection from the present moment of every "me" who has ever lived down to the dawn of creation.

The third kind of individualism which is so prevalent in contemporary Western Christian culture that we need to guard ourselves against, as also already noted, is individualism with respect to *responsibility*—the idea that our relationship with God is something that we, by our individual faithfulness toward God, are primarily responsible for accomplishing and sustaining independent of the faithfulness of God (and others) toward us. However, what is so important we understand is that the thing that accomplishes and sustains our relationship with God is not something we achieve by our own rugged Christian individualism and religious exertions. Our being incorporated into the love of God is a gift and enabling that we receive from God through the power of God's Holy Spirit. Although it is certainly true that what God has done for us by grace through Jesus Christ requires a human response from us, it is not our human response that *accomplishes* and *sustains* all that we enjoy in God. Our right relationship with God always remains something that is secured for us in and through Jesus Christ and made available to us by God's Holy Spirit. It is the free gift of God's grace, by which we are enabled to flourish as the true people God has created us to be.

As we reflect on these three individualisms in light of the biblical truth that God *is* love and seeks our participation *in* God's love, it becomes clear that it is God's desire and intention to draw—not just isolated individuals disconnected from the networks of relationships that constitute them as authentic persons—but *all* humanity and *all* creation into the loving relationality of Father, Son, and Holy Spirit. Therefore, it is God's desire that all humanity and all creation not only be in fellowship with God as *individuals*—but in fellowship with *each other* and with *all creation* also. This is because fellowship and right relationship with God is never something God calls us to pursue as some kind of privatized blessing in isolation from fellowship and right relationship with others. Neither is it something we can pursue in isolation from fellowship and right relationship with God's creation.

The prayer of Jesus in John 17 reveals that God has come to us in and as Jesus Christ to invite and enable us to participate in the love of God as fellow lovers and as those who are loved. It reveals that God is a relational God of intimacy and oneness, yet also a God who creates freedom and space for us to participate in a history of encounter—the end purpose of which is that we learn to know God and to enjoy him. Moreover, God has created us to be relational beings because it is only as genuinely relational beings that we are enabled to enjoy relationships of love that are authentically *human*—with God, with ourselves, with each other, and with the world.

What flows out of this is that love is not only a description of *God's* inner being and outward desire—it is also a description of *our* very human being and purpose, and thus a description of our hearts' deepest yearning and need. Love is therefore a description of the very essence of what God has created us to be as human beings created in God's image and likeness. It inevitably follows that love is something we long for in *our* relationships also. As human beings we long for relationships of love in which we can enjoy closeness and intimacy in relationship with those who are external to us, yet at the same time receive the freedom and space whereby our distinctive personhood as individuals is safeguarded, honored, and enabled to flourish.

Because God is a relational God who has made us to be relational beings for the purpose of relationship with him, with one another, and with the world; this means that all the biblical concepts that describe these relationships must be understood primarily in relational terms. However, because the three kinds of individualism we have discussed are so prevalent within contemporary Western Christian culture, this unfortunately predisposes us to think *behaviorally* rather than *relationally*—that is, in terms of ourselves as individuals and what it is that we *do*, rather than in terms of how we are connected to others. Or if we do think relationally our tendency is to elevate and prioritize behavior *over* relationship. I would go so far as to say that if we could learn to consistently think relationally and therefore to consistently elevate and prioritize relationship over behavior, this would be utterly transformational to our Christian worship and witness in the world, our health and well-being, and our joy in life.

In this chapter I want to begin to explore what I consider to be the beating heart that lies at the center of my whole project—our great need to think relationally about the God who *is* the God of loving relationality who has created us as relational beings for the purpose of relationship with God, with ourselves, with others, and with the world.

Traditional Christian ways of thinking and speaking about the relationship God has with humanity very often give the impression that God's acceptance and love is based on some sort of contractual transaction in response to our ongoing faithfulness and obedience toward God. In other words, that our relationship with God is primarily a matter of *our behavior*. In light of this I find it profoundly insightful that Voyle should speak of our great need to

> awaken to the reality that we are *already enfolded in [God's] eternal loving-kindness* [which] liberates us from this fundamental fear [that we may never gain love or, having gained it, we will lose it] and sets us free to manifest that eternal love in this temporal world.[3]

The expression "loving-kindness" is frequently chosen by translators for rendering into English the Hebrew word *chesed*. God's *chesed* is God's determination to *be* in the external world the kind of god that from all eternity God *is* within his triune self—the God who *is* love. God's *chesed* is God's faithfulness and integrity toward his triune self as Father, Son, and Holy Spirit; and flowing from this faithfulness, to be faithful to all that he has created and purposed. God's *chesed* therefore is the outward expression of the loving relationality of Father, Son, and Holy Spirit through which God seeks the participation of all creation in God's love. In this way God's

---

3. Voyle, "Appreciative Inquiry," 125, emphasis added.

chesed is a *relational* thing that generates a *behavioral* outworking in the external reality God has created. So instead of translating *chesed* as "loving-kindness," it is sometimes translated "covenantal faithfulness" or "mercy," or sometimes simply "love."

But in our individualistic, value-oriented consumer culture we are so prone to thinking about our relationships in terms of *conditionality* and *reciprocity*—these both being contractual and behavioral terms. It is often the case that children who have been raised in a contract mentality environment feel they have never been genuinely loved, accepted, and celebrated simply for who they are. They feel that their receiving love, affirmation, and acceptance is always conditional upon satisfying their parents' expectations or behaving in ways that reciprocate sufficiently well their parents' behavior toward them. This inevitably produces feelings of anxiety and insecurity—these children always wondering if they have behaved well enough to merit their parents' approval. Or as Voyle puts it:

> When loving or getting love is the focus of our activity, we will actually live in fear, afraid that we may never gain love or, having gained it, we will lose it.[4]

This contract behavior mentality is so pervasive in our Western culture that we are in grave danger of bringing this same mentality to our relationship with God. We are at risk of believing that our receiving God's love and acceptance is based on some sort of contract—that God's approval of us is conditional upon our giving value to God, our satisfying God's expectations, and us behaving in ways that reciprocate sufficiently well the infinite goodness of God toward us. However, when we bring a contract behavior mentality to our relationship with God what actually happens is that we become *pagans*—that is, we become religiously motivated people who think that God, if approached in the right way, may be willing to cut a deal with us or may even be open to accepting bribes. In other words, we become people who believe that if we give God something we think *God* values (like worship and zealous faithfulness) or which costs us something (like sacrifice and devoted obedience) then God will give us something that *we* value (like approval and abundant blessing).

But the true God and Father of our Lord Jesus Christ is *not* a pagan god! This means that God doesn't want us to have a pagan contract mentality relationship with him. What we must understand is that God's relationship

---

4. Voyle, "Appreciative Inquiry," 125.

with us is never established on the basis of *contract*; rather God's relationships are always established on the basis of *covenant*. A contract is a commercial relationship that is established by negotiation between two parties who agree to behave conditionally and reciprocally toward each other in order to facilitate the exchange of mutually advantageous value. But a covenant is a personal relationship that is established at God's gracious initiative by coming to a person or a people of God's own choosing and declaring to them, "This is the kind of God I will be to you and this is the kind of people you will be to me." This means that God's covenants are completely one-sided from the point of view of their establishment. God never consults us or negotiates with us as if God imagines we have something of value we might bring to the table. Every covenant God establishes with his human creatures is always at God's initiative, always on God's terms, and is always an expression of God's desire to bring people into loving relationship with himself—the God who *is* love. Moreover, every covenant God establishes has this shape—God declaring, as Jeremiah 31:33 puts it:

> I will be their God and they will be my people.

The nearest analogy from our human experience by which we can understand God's covenant of grace is the relationship we have with our children. We never consult our children to see if they agree to be born to us. We don't negotiate terms with them before consenting to conceive them. We don't stipulate minimum acceptable behavioral requirements that we require of them in order for them to uphold their side of the agreement. Instead, as parents, we covenant ourselves to our children in love long before they can even respond to us—perhaps even before they are conceived. We covenant ourselves to our children in love that we will be their mother and father and love them no matter what—irrespective of their behavior. In bringing them into the world we, in effect, declare to them, "We will be your parents and you will be our child."

In saying to our children, "I will be your father," or, "I will be your mother," what we are really saying is, "This is the kind of person I promise to be toward you—I solemnly promise that I will love you and care for you and be there for you no matter what." When we say, "And you will be our child," we are really saying exactly the same thing; but additionally we are saying that we expect their behavior toward us to correspond to our covenantal love toward them. In other words, we expect them to behave in ways that harmonize with and affirm the relationship of loving-kindness we have with them in order that we both may find joy in participating in and experiencing this love together in genuinely relational ways.

Nevertheless, in all this the relationship we have with our children is always a *covenantal relationship* and never a *behavioral contract*. This means that although we expect their behavior to correspond to our relationship with them, their behavior is never made to be the foundational basis or causal reason for this relationship. Rather, their behavior shapes the way the covenantal relationship of love we have with them is enjoyed. Moreover, and most importantly, the truth about our relationship with our children is that in coming into the world they are *already* enfolded in our loving-kindness! Consequently, their great task (and ours to guide them in this) is not that they, by their *behavior*, try to find or win our love by making themselves attractive or good enough for us to open the door of our heart to them, but rather, as they grow and develop they become aware of, learn to trust as true, and enter into the *relationship* of love that already surrounds them so that they may participate in this relationship with us as fully functioning persons in their own right and integrity of being.

What this means therefore is that our behavior can never create or destroy God's covenantal relationship of love with us. Nevertheless, God is very interested in our behavior. This is because our behavior shapes the way God behaves toward us in his covenantal love. In other words, our behavior influences the way our relationship with God is enjoyed—or perhaps *not* enjoyed. God's covenantal love for us is such that God will never accept behavior from us that threatens to destroy us or others and therefore God's covenantal love is a *righteous* and *wrathful* love. God always seeks our highest good and greatest joy and so, in love, God teaches us, corrects us, encourages us, rebukes us, affirms us, disciplines us, and guides us—always with the goal of building Christlikeness in us in order to enlarge our capacity to experience more fully the covenantal relationship of love that God has called us into.

Again, the nearest analogy we have from our human experience that allows us to understand God's covenantal, righteous, wrathful love is a mother's love—a mother's love for the child that has been conceived, grown, and developed within her womb; been born to her through suffering; and suckled at her breast—a mother's love that has raised her child the best she can through all the different stages and circumstances of their lives together. At somewhat more of a distance, but still near enough to see and understand, this is something a *father* can relate to also. Consequently, as parents of the children we love, we know *our* righteous, wrathful anger against all that would endanger our children—all that might threaten them and cause them to become opposed to being the good people God intends for them to become, whether these threats come from some external source or from within their own foolish, childish imaginations and perverse choices. As parents of the children we love we are therefore able to understand this kind of relational, righteous, wrathful love. Therefore we can readily understand that this powerful parental *anger* that seeks to protect and safeguard our children from harm is in fact the flip side of our powerful parental *love* that arises out of our deep desire for relationship—that is, our parental relationship of powerful love that desires our children have life in all its fullness and abundance in right relationship with us and in right relationship with God, with themselves, with others, and with the world.

Moreover, and most importantly, it is precisely *God's* covenantal, righteous, wrathful love for us that reveals the truth concerning who *we* truly are as human beings—that God is our heavenly mother and father. This is because who else but a loving parent can ever be righteously wrathful in *this* way? Consequently, the revelation of God's covenantal, wrathful, righteous love for us is the revelation concerning who *we* truly are—that we are *God's children*.

This means that God's righteous wrath is always God's wrathful *love* and never his wrathful *hate*. God's righteous wrath is not human wrath. God's wrath is revealed in the gospel of Jesus Christ, which is God's power to save all who believe, and it is therefore not revealed by punishing people with fire from heaven for being "sinners." Rather, God's righteous wrath is revealed in the gospel, which is God's power to reconcile to himself and draw into loving relationship precisely these very people. In this way God's righteous wrath is the shadow side of his saving love—it is God's "no" that God speaks *to* us and *against* us, but only for the sake of his "yes" that God speaks *to* us and *for* us. God's covenantal, righteous, wrathful love is therefore God's judgment concerning who we truly are, what we have become on account of the temporary aberration of sin, and what we shall be again in the redemptive purposes of God. God's covenantal, righteous, wrathful love is therefore God's condemnation and destruction of our sinful humanity in Jesus Christ, and in this way God's judgment in the crucifixion and resurrection of Jesus Christ that we all must die—*in order that we all may truly live!* God's righteous, wrathful, love therefore is God's grace and the redemption and restoration of our true humanity in Jesus Christ.

What this means, therefore, is that as human beings we are what we are because God has created us for relationships of love—with God, with ourselves, with one another, and with the world. God has therefore placed deep within our beings a frighteningly powerful instinct that responds to the deep hurt of broken relationships. The way our relational hurts penetrate to the very core of our beings; the way our emotional responses react to this hurt with such powerful passion; and how all this so often impacts upon us in such profoundly dysfunctional ways are all indicators of just how central to our very beings loving relationships are to us. The truth is that this frighteningly powerful instinct within us corresponds to, *and bears witness to*, the wonderfully powerful covenantal love that God has for us and God's desire that we behave faithfully in the relationships into which he calls us.

2

Faith
—so whose faith saves who?

IN THE PREVIOUS CHAPTER we saw that God is a relational god who has created us as relational beings in order that we may enjoy relationship with God, with ourselves, with one another, and with the world. We also saw that God's covenantal love toward us is primarily a relational thing that gives rise to behavioral actions on God's part toward us—actions that derive from, and correspond to, the primary relational fact that God is our heavenly mother and father. This means that all the key terms that describe this relationship must be understood relationally. We have already seen this with the foundational term "love" but this is also true of all the other key terms that describe this relationship, such as "faith," "sin," "righteousness," and "salvation." What this means therefore is that our faith in God is primarily a relational thing that gives rise to behavioral actions toward God that derive from, and correspond to, the fact that we are God's children.

In Romans 1:16–17 the Apostle Paul says:

> For I am not ashamed of the gospel: it is the power of God for salvation to everyone who has faith, to the Jew first and also to the Greek. For in it the righteousness of God is revealed through faith for faith; as it is written, "He who through faith is righteous shall live." (NRSV)

Many Christians read this and assume that Paul is speaking of *our* faith in God. This is reinforced by translations that render his curious expression "through faith for faith" as "faith from first to last." What is often assumed here is that Paul is saying we have to have faith in God from first to last in order to avail ourselves of God's saving mercy toward us through Jesus Christ.

But the point Paul is making is that the originating fact that stands at the heart and center of God's saving power to all who believe, and which reveals God's righteousness, is not primarily *our* faith in God at all—rather it is *God's* faithfulness toward us. Or more correctly, it is God's *chesed*— God's faithfulness in which from all eternity God has freely chosen in love to bind himself in covenantal love toward Godself as Father, Son, and Holy Spirit *in order that we might have life in God*. It is precisely this covenantal faithfulness of God that Paul calls God's *righteousness*.

The point Paul is making with this expression "through faith for faith" or "from out of faith into faith" is that our being made relationally right with God comes "through" or "from out of" God's *chesed* faithfulness to be and do what God has promised from all eternity to be and do. Moreover, in order for us to know, live in, and experience God's life-giving saving grace in genuinely relational ways it is necessary for us to respond to God's faithfulness toward us with our own faith in God. This is what Paul means by "for faith" or "into faith."

We know this to be true in any relationship. It is of little value knowing in an abstract, theoretical kind of way that someone loves us if we don't actually interact with them in genuinely relational ways that enable us to come to know and trust them such that we freely choose to participate in their love for us by loving them in return. Therefore in order for us to experience and participate in the reality of someone's love it is necessary for us to respond to the one who loves us with our own love for them. In our relationship with God our relational response to *God's* faithfulness toward us is *our* faith in God. Therefore our faith is our secondary behavioral human response to God's primary relational action of covenantal faithfulness toward us. This is what Paul means by this strange expression, "through faith for faith." It really means:

> The gospel is God's power to save all who believe [and this embraces all people no matter who] for in the gospel the righteousness [or covenantal *chesed* faithfulness] of God is revealed originating through [or from out of] God's faithfulness toward us and finding its intended human response for [or into] our faith in God.

In this way it really is faith from first to last. At the beginning stands the faithfulness of God—God's covenantal *chesed* faithfulness to be and do all that God has purposed and promised to be and do to reconcile all humanity and all creation to himself in love, by grace in and through Jesus Christ by the power of God's Holy Spirit—and our receiving, benefiting from, and participating in this love through our own response of faith in God.

To picture this it helps to imagine a long arc that has its beginning in God's triune covenantal *chesed* faithfulness from before the beginning of creation, and this arc reaching out, spanning all space, time, and eternity, seeking a human response—seeking our answering "yes" and "amen" toward God as our fitting response to God's "yes" and "let it be so" toward us. Our fitting human response to *God's* faithfulness toward us is *our* faith in God.

But the truth is that the fitting *human* response to God's "yes" and "let it be so" toward us in its primary and foundational sense is not actually *our* faith in God at all—it is the faithfulness of Jesus Christ. The truly fitting human response to God's "yes" in all its fullness is the covenantal faithfulness of Jesus Christ on our behalf as the one true human in whose humanity and personhood our own humanity and personhood is constituted by God's grace. This means that the faith that saves us is the faith of Jesus Christ for us and on our behalf. Consequently this is not something that comes *from us* in its primary and originating sense at all—rather it is God's gift of grace *from* God *to* us. This is what Paul is getting at in Ephesians 2:8:

> For it is by grace you have been saved, through faith—and this is not from yourselves, it is the gift of God—not by works, so that no one can boast.

It is often the case that when Christians think about faith they think first in terms of *content*. In other words, they think about certain biblical *teachings* or theological *propositions* or doctrinal *statements* they are required to believe as being objectively true. But this sort of thing only comes second. Actually, it only comes *third*. Genuine Christian faith is first and foremost *relational*. Consequently it is not primarily belief in statements *about* God, rather it is a relationship of trust *in* God as our fitting human response to God's saving faithfulness toward us. Genuine Christian faith therefore consists of three distinct although connected components:

1. First and foremost Christian faith is a *relationship with God* that God initiates through the enabling power of God's Holy Spirit, in which we learn to put our trust in God's covenantal *chesed* faithfulness and saving mercy toward us in Jesus Christ.

2. Second, flowing out of this primary relationship of trust in God, faith is *Christian behavior* that corresponds to and bears faithful witness to this primary relationship of trust—our human behavior that gives confirming evidence that our relationship of trust we have in God's relational faithfulness and saving mercy toward us in Jesus Christ is authentic. That is, behavior that seeks to actualize in our lives, in genuinely relational ways, God's faithfulness to us.

3. Third, flowing out of this relationship in which our trust in God's relational faithfulness and saving mercy toward us in Jesus Christ is shown to be authentic by our Christian behavior, as we journey with God we learn that certain things about God are objectively true and others are not. This is where Christian faith concerning *doctrinal beliefs* comes in.

There are two common misunderstandings regarding the nature of faith that causes so much distress and unhappiness and which have the potential to infect every aspect of Christian worship and witness. The first misunderstanding arises out of a failure to maintain these three aspects of faith in their correct *order*, and therefore arises when we fail to give primacy to faith as a relationship of trust in God's covenantal *chesed* faithfulness.

This first misunderstanding is getting the *order* of these three different aspects of faith muddled up and thinking that it is our right behavior toward God (number 2) that takes priority over, and therefore determines, our right relationship with God (number 1). This is what lies at the root of so much Christian insecurity, legalism, religious superstition, and fear—thinking that it is our *behavior toward God* that secures and safeguards *our relationship with God* and that it is this right behavior that establishes the basis upon which we are permitted to enjoy God's loving acceptance and blessing. Or alternatively it is thinking that it is our belief in right doctrines about God (number 3) that takes priority over, and therefore determines, our right relationship with God (number 1). This is what lies at the root of so much Christian distrust of others, controversy, denominationalism, and sectarian hostility—thinking that it is our believing *correct doctrines about God* that secures and safeguards our *relationship with God*.

Let me illustrate. In my early twenties I was full of all the excitement and certainty and insecurity of being a zealous young Christian. I think this partly reflected the church I attended at the time—it also was young, exciting, zealous, certain, and insecure. One Sunday, one of the preachers gave a sermon about how he was walking to church one day and how he was generally feeling excited and certain and zealous. But as he walked that happy morning he suddenly became very insecure. He had noticed a discarded pornographic magazine in the gutter and his first instinct was to want to look at the pictures—and he felt utterly undone! He felt vile and sinful and hypocritical. In his shame he felt a complete Christian fraud. He only told this story much later after he had pulled himself together in order to preach a message about how deceitful sin is and how corrupt and defiled we humans are.

Yet even as a young Christian somehow I instinctively knew that something just didn't ring true in this. As I recall this story now as an older Christian, what I believe was going on was that this minister thought that his behavior that morning *didn't* bear faithful witness to the authenticity of his relationship of trust with God. He thought that being tempted to look at the magazine (and then feeling bad about this) meant that this was evidence that his relationship with God was *inauthentic*. So he felt hypocritical, guilt-ridden, and miserable.

In other words, what I think happened was that he got the *order* wrong. He thought (I suspect subconsciously) that his right behavior toward God (number 2) took priority over, and in this way determined, his right relationship with God (number 1). He thought therefore that the kind of behavior that *would* confirm his faith as authentically Christian was a kind of Christian piety that was so high and holy and sinless that it meant, in effect, he was sufficiently good enough on his own account to no longer need God's saving mercy! Even as a young Christian I thought—surely the kind of behavior that *is* consistent with Christian faith is the kind of behavior that authentically bears witness to the truth about us; namely, that we are maintained in right relationship with God and continue *to be* maintained in right relationship with God only by God's gracious mercy whereby God, in covenantal faithfulness, continually reminds and assures us that we are *already* and therefore *always* enfolded in God's eternal loving-kindness— and therefore *not* by our pious religious behavior.

In my view, the lesson this preacher should have taught us from his story was that when he had that sudden desire to look at the magazine he should have laughed at himself and thanked God, saying, "Lord, I believe, help my unbelief! Yet again I am reminded just how much I live by your covenantal saving mercy"—and then got on about his business instead of wallowing in spiritual self-pity. This is because genuine Christian faith is first and foremost a *relationship of trust* in God in which we come to know and believe that God really does love us and delight in us and that there is nothing in all creation that is ever going to separate us from God's love.

What should flow out of this is that this sets us free to be emotionally and spiritually honest with ourselves, with God, and with one another about who we truly are—in God and in ourselves. Of all the religious sins we are capable of committing perhaps the most toxic is our being emotionally dishonest and spiritually inauthentic—our thinking that Christian *faith* really means Christian *perfection* and therefore (inevitably) the practice of Christian *pretence* whereby we feel compelled to enact before others something we know we are not.

It is so important we understand that we are incorporated into right relationship with God—not by our religious or moral behavior toward God—but by God's covenantal *chesed* faithfulness toward us. The truth about us is that we are a bundle of contradictions—that, yes, it is true that in Jesus Christ the old is gone and the new has come, but that it is also true that God's new creation in us has not yet been revealed in all its fullness. The truth about us is that God *accepts* us as we are, but doesn't want us to *remain* as we are. The truth about us is that God has called us into a genuine relationship of love and so this means it is a relationship in which God always respects our freedom and integrity, and so there will be times, whether in ignorance or in disobedience or in sheer *humanness*, that we revert to some of our old ways. Nevertheless when we *do* revert and *do* behave badly—and *feel* bad because of this—this also is evidence and confirmation that our relationship with God is genuine. It is evidence that we really do care about our relationship with God and that we really do want to live better for God. It is evidence of the work of God's Spirit in our lives prompting us to hear yet again God's gracious word that we are *already* and therefore *always* enfolded in God's eternal loving-kindness.

This means that we can rejoice even in our sins! This is because our sins demonstrate to us how much we still *need*, and therefore can *claim*, the life-changing power of God's saving grace. But please note carefully—we don't rejoice *that* we commit sins and nor do we commit sins so that God's grace toward us might increase. Nevertheless the truth is that we can rejoice even in our sinful behavior. In order to help us, therefore, God gives us his Holy Spirit who creates within us the *desire* and gives us the *enabling* to behave better in ways that authentically bear faithful witness to the relationship we have with God. What we must understand however is that none of this behavior—whether good or bad—is the *cause* or *basis* of our relationship with God. The cause of our relationship with God is always God's covenantal *chesed* faithfulness toward us—not our faithful behavioral response toward God.

The second misunderstanding concerning Christian faith arises out of a failure to maintain a clear *separation* and *distinction* between these three aspects of faith and therefore to *fuse* them together (and in this way *confuse* them) and so treat them as being one and the same thing. It arises out of thinking that our right behavior toward God (number 2) is identically equivalent to our right relationship with God (number 1) and thus our believing that for us to behave badly or to experience unworthy thoughts and feelings or to discover aspects about ourselves that stand in contradiction to established Christian norms must inevitably threaten our relationship with God. This is what lies at the root of so much Christian smug superiority, elitism, and moral judgmentalism toward others (if we are satisfied with our behavior) or else so much fear, insecurity, shame, and pretence (if we are not). Alternatively it is thinking that our right doctrinal beliefs about God (number 3) are identically equivalent to our right relationship with God (number 1) and thus believing that to think and speak wrongly about God or to critically question our theology concerning God must inevitably threaten our relationship with God. This is what lies at the root of so much Christian failure of fellowship with those who think differently about God and so much "plastic" spiritual inauthenticity by which we suppress our doubts around what we believe to be true about God.

Now in this same church as a zealous young Christian, full of excitement and certainty and insecurity (this is to illustrate this second misunderstanding concerning faith), I became aware there were certain doctrines that were *taboo* and couldn't be questioned. One of these doctrines was the conviction that the group I belonged to at this time were the only true Christians! I quickly picked up the vibe that you just didn't ask this question—that to question this doctrine would threaten your relationship with the group and therefore with God also. Moreover I came to realize that other people secretly questioned this doctrine too, but didn't voice it because they were frightened. Somehow I instinctively knew that something in this didn't ring true either.

This second misunderstanding concerning faith means that it is important to keep these three aspects of faith distinct from each other and not fuse them together. Therefore we must never imagine that our *relationship with God* is identically the same thing as our *doctrinal beliefs about God*. The easiest way to sum this up is to say, "We are not our theologies!" My theology is the thoughts I have about God and the words and ideas I use to try and express them. Clearly my theology has a big influence upon how I behave—and so it should. But who I am in my relationship with God is not one and the same thing as my thoughts about God and the words and illustrations I use to try and express these thoughts.

The problem with this thing about taboo doctrines that must never be questioned is that for many Christians these two aspects of faith *are* one and the same thing—they think that if the ideas they have about God and the words they use to express these ideas are threatening to the group's theology then this must threaten their relationship with God. What this mistaken thinking does is hold people in fear, insecurity, and silence such that the honest and open exchange of thoughts, doubts, and ideas about God never genuinely takes place. Consequently (and perversely) it produces a kind of false certainty in which people feel compelled to make confident doctrinal statements about God in order to allay this underlying insecurity.

However, when we are able to keep our theology distinct from our identity, and therefore our relationship of trusting faith in God distinct from our theological beliefs about God (and not fall into the trap of thinking they are one and the same thing) this gives us wonderful freedom and confidence to be honest with God, honest with ourselves, and honest with each other. It gives us the life-giving freedom to ask questions *of* God and *about* God—all the while knowing that this will never threaten our relationship *with* God.

Imagine a child with her father or mother thinking that her relationship with her parents is identically the same as her thoughts and speech about them. Therefore in order to be secure in her parents' love for her, she must only ever think and say "correct" things about them. Surely we can see how unhealthy this must be—how insecure and inauthentic the relationship would become. On the other hand imagine a child with her father or mother knowing that her relationship with them is completely secure—that she is *already* and therefore *always* enfolded in their loving-kindness and there is nothing in all creation that can separate her from her parents' love. This relationship of trust provides the firm foundation upon which she has the freedom to think and ask questions—*and also make mistakes*—and in this way learn. Clearly this is a much more healthy, secure, and authentic relationship.

Now imagine that *God* is your loving father and mother—no, better still—actually *trust* that God really *is* your loving heavenly mother and father and that you are God's much-loved child. Imagine you are walking together knowing you are enfolded in God's eternal loving-kindness and that your mind is filled with the wonder and the mystery of this. Imagine God invites you, as Jesus invited his disciples, saying, "Who do you say that I am?" In the security you have in relationship with God and out of the curiosity you have concerning the vastness and mystery of God you begin to think and speak. You search for words and metaphors and illustrations to express your thoughts about God and the questions you want to ask. Do you really imagine God expects you to get an A+ theologically correct answer every time—or even *at all*? Of course not! There has never been a theologian worthy of God and there is never going to be one. Nevertheless God loves our thoughts about him—not because they are necessarily theologically correct or doctrinally sound, but because we think and say them in childlike trusting love. God loves our thoughts about him because we think them out of a genuine desire to know God better and because we are willing to learn from God and to think and speak better of God as we have opportunity to learn.

3

Sinners
—so who are we speaking to?

IN CALLING HIS FIRST disciples, Jesus doesn't seem overly concerned about getting the sin message across. He simply says, "Follow me"—and they start doing life together and bearing witness to the nearness of God's kingdom. Yet when *we* seek to make disciples for Jesus we generally assume that a key priority is to speak about human sin as soon as possible. Why is this? Take any typical Christian evangelistic tract. More often than not after trying to find some point of common ground it will get down to its real Christian business along the following lines:

> God is Holy: "For all have sinned and come short of the glory of God" (Rom 3:23). We have all broken God's law. God cannot tolerate our sin. He must punish it. God is Just: "For the wages of sin is death" (Rom 6:23). God's law says that death is the punishment for sin.

These tracts will go on to speak of God being *loving* and *gracious* and *forgiving*, but notice the order—almost invariably the first task is to get the sin message across.

As I have emphasized in my introduction, the thing that really struck me about Rob Voyle's *Appreciative Inquiry Paradigm* is his statement:

> When a person is continually shamed over a period of time, the shamed person will be motivated to destroy those who are shaming them.

When I read these words they struck me like a prophetic thunderclap. Could it be that people removing themselves from and seeking to destroy Christian influence in the world is actually a natural human response to an institution that for far too long has focused on what is wrong with people by addressing them as "sinners"? As I consider this I am convinced that God is calling us to rethink our Christian conviction that presenting the good news about Jesus means we have to tell people at the earliest possible opportunity that "all [and especially *them*] have sinned and fallen short of the glory of God."

It is increasingly clear to me that as the Christendom paradigm has waned in the West the vast majority of *non-* and *used-to-be*-Christians simply no longer recognize themselves in our traditional descriptions of them.

> I work hard, I love my family, I pay my taxes [they respond]. I know I'm not perfect, but I haven't murdered or raped anyone. But you seem to be saying that God's fundamental orientation toward me is anger and condemnation because I'm "a sinner." But I think that in demanding perfect law-obedience your god is petty and pedantic—what genuinely authentic relationship involving human beings is ever sustained on the basis of *perfection*? Moreover the idea that this god of yours will consign me to everlasting punishment in hell if I don't believe in Jesus is morally repugnant—what sort of "loving father" would do that? What's more—I simply cannot see how killing Jesus on the cross has anything to do with love or the "sin" problem you say that I have. And tell me this—what use is a "pie in the sky" salvation that only has value when I *die*?

The more I think about this the more I wonder if the thing that really *has* fallen short of the glory of God is not so much the behavior of "sinners" out there—but *our Christian understanding of Jesus and his gospel!*

In order to rethink this commonly accepted Christian approach to speaking of the good news of Jesus, I believe we need to begin by asking what might seem a rather strange question—"Who are we speaking to?"[1]

---

1. In this, and the following two chapters, I am drawing on what I consider to be three of the most important insights from the theology of Karl Barth. Namely: (1) our true humanity is constituted not in ourselves, but in Jesus Christ (*Church Dogmatics* III/2, *The Doctrine of Creation*); (2) we must understand sin, not from the context of our human being, but the saving work of Jesus Christ in which sin's claim upon us is already defeated (*Church Dogmatics* IV/1, *The Doctrine of Reconciliation*); and (3) God's election is not of individuals, but rather, Jesus Christ is both the electing God and the elected human in whom our election as individuals is constituted (*Church Dogmatics* II/2, *The Doctrine of God*).

The church of Jesus is called to proclaim the gospel to all people, but, *who* precisely is the person God calls us to address? As far as I can tell, the person most Christians assume God calls us to address is—"a sinner." This assumption has been the driving force behind most Protestant evangelical proclamation over the last five hundred years—that we are to preach *law* in order to highlight *sin* thus creating *guilt* so as to encourage *repentance* and in this way prepare people to receive *God's gracious acceptance* and forgiveness through *faith* in Jesus Christ.

However, I believe we need to rethink this, and I want to do this by asking my question slightly differently—"Who is the person God has created to be God's partner, child, and friend?" "Who is the true human God has planned from all eternity to love, give freedom to, and be in relationship with?" As I read the Bible, the true human God seeks to be in fellowship with is *not* a sinner; it is the true human we see in Jesus Christ. Consider what the Apostle Paul says concerning this in Galatians 2:20:

> I have been crucified with Christ and I no longer live, but Christ lives in me. The life I now live in the body, I live by faith in the Son of God, who loved me and gave himself for me.

The true human Paul speaks of here—the true *I* who "lives by faith in the Son of God"—is clearly *not* Paul the sinner because *that* Paul is dead, crucified with Christ. Rather, the Paul God has planned from all eternity to be in fellowship with is the true Paul we see in Jesus Christ. As he says:

> I no longer live, but Christ lives in me.

Therefore I am convinced that it is *this* person, this true human in Jesus Christ, we are called to acknowledge, address, and affirm as we share the good news of God's grace with others.

In Romans 7:20 this same Paul says:

> Now if I do what I do not want to do, it is no longer I who do it, but it is sin living in me that does it.

Here, as he also does in Galatians, Paul refers to two different *I*'s—two different beings. The first is an *I* who genuinely wants to do the good and right thing—the true Paul. But there is a second—another being who we thoughtlessly also call *I* who lives in contradiction to what our true *I* wants—a concealed being who masquerades as the real me, who bewilders and shames me by its actions, but who in truth is an imposter whose true identity remains hidden. Moreover, it is precisely because this being remains concealed in plain sight, hidden and unrecognized, that it is free to do all manner of perversity in my name and then shift the blame back on me! But as Paul says, the true identity of this false impostor *I* is *not* the real *me*, but rather:

> It is the sin living in me that does it.

This is my point—when we address people as "sinners" we are actually talking to the wrong person! We are addressing them as if it is this "imposter within" who is in fact the real them. Therefore in addressing people as sinners, instead of speaking to the true human God has created to be God's partner, child, and friend, we are in fact addressing the imposter within whose great work consists in trying to keep them from *recognizing, accepting*, and *incarnating* their true humanity in Jesus! When we address people as "sinners" this reinforces the impression that God declares (and we Christians also believe) that the "true them" really is a bad person—that their *bad behavior* has determined their *true being*. It is precisely this that creates the shame and the desire of shamed people to want to alienate themselves from or else destroy that which is shaming them.

We see this most clearly with children. When we confront children about their bad behavior so often in their shame they believe that this bad person we point to is in fact the real them which then becomes their truth they learn to live in obedience to. Consequently, in a perverse inversion of the incarnation, instead of God's living Word of grace becoming flesh in order to be God with them and for them; our word of condemnation becomes flesh in them and they respond by incarnating this shame within themselves. Moreover, the great tragedy is that if they genuinely come to believe that the true source of their shame is *themselves* then the thing they become motivated to alienate themselves from or else destroy will be *themselves*!

There is a deeply moving scene in *Les Misérables* and it comes out even more strongly in the novel by Victor Hugo. Jean Valjean, who has been imprisoned for stealing, has become a brute of a man: brutalized and dehumanized by the law that can only ever address him in terms of what he has done wrong—with the label "convict" that the law forces him to wear. This is reinforced by the zealous administration of this convict-making law through the policeman Javert, who in my reading represents the church which needs to rethink its theological conviction that its evangelistic task is to confront people with their sin at the earliest possible opportunity.

Upon his release, having served his time, Valjean is forced to continue living under this law—under the judgment that his *sinful behavior* has determined his *true being*. He therefore grows to hate this system that can only ever shame and dehumanise him by pointing to what is wrong in him and he is consequently motivated to alienate himself from it or else destroy it. He therefore breaks his parole and escapes. In desperate need he finds sanctuary with an old priest who gives him welcome and hospitality. However, Valjean, still thinking himself to be the brute the law has defined him as being, steals from the priest. But to his utter amazement receives from the old priest—not condemnation on account of his sinful behavior—but gracious mercy on account of his true humanity in Jesus Christ. The thing that finally reaches into and transforms Valjean, causing him to recognize and accept as real his true self and which brings about his repentance, was that the old priest acknowledged, addressed, and affirmed him as a true man—he called him "Monsieur." In other words the old priest didn't address him as "a sinner"—the way the *law* did and only ever could. Rather, he addressed him according to his true humanity in Jesus Christ.

It is so important we Christians understand this. The truth is, sin is so toxic and so destructive that we cannot safely or responsibly speak of it outside of the grace of God, in which it is already named and exposed and its claim upon us already defeated in Jesus Christ—and therefore from that place of grace where all condemnation is already removed. But when we speak of sin in the context of our human being outside of the grace of God (that is, by addressing people as "sinners"), sin can only ever do what it only ever does—it brings forth condemnation, shame, and death.

However, it is so very important we don't misunderstand this as meaning that we are to *never* speak to people concerning what is wrong. Rather, everything hinges upon the *context* within which we speak of our universal wrongness: this thing we call "sin." I believe Jesus models this for us in the story of the woman accused of adultery in John 8.

> Teacher, this woman was caught in the act of adultery. In the Law, Moses commanded us to stone such a woman. Now, what do you say?

We should notice first what Jesus *does*. John tells us that he wrote on the ground with his finger. Curiously, most Bible commentators at this point speculate on *what* Jesus wrote. But John's point is not *what* he wrote, but *that* he wrote—and that he did so with his *finger*—and that he did so *twice!* This action of Jesus is an enacted parable that recalls that twice in the Old

Testament we encounter a finger that writes—first, the Ten Commandments in Deuteronomy 9:10 (words of divine *command*) and second, the judgment upon King Belshazzar in Daniel 5 (words of divine *judgment*). Here, therefore, in a very real context of zealous religious humans attempting to interpret words of divine command and apply words of divine judgment, Jesus enacts a silent parable for those who have eyes to see that demonstrates that it is he himself who in his very being: *is* God's living Word of revelation; *is* the law and the prophets; *is* both law-giver and judge; and therefore *is* God's living Word of divine command and divine judgment! Therefore in the presence of Jesus both the law of Moses and all human judgment must concede ground to him!

After Jesus says to her accusers that it is only the one who is without sin who possesses the moral authority necessary to throw the first stone, John tells us in 8:9–11:

> At this, those who heard began to go away one at a time, the older ones first, until only Jesus was left, with the woman still standing there. Jesus straightened up and asked her, "Woman, where are they? Has no one condemned you?" "No one, sir," she said. "Then neither do I condemn you," Jesus declared. "Go now and leave your life of sin."

But notice what Jesus *doesn't* say. He doesn't say, "Neither do I condemn you, God loves you just the way you are—go now and don't change a thing." It is true that God welcomes us and loves us just as we are. It is true therefore that God *loves* us in our sin. But God does not *leave* us in our sin! In welcoming us and loving us God does not treat us as though there is nothing wrong with us—as though there is nothing about us that needs to be healed, cleansed, changed, and repented of. Jesus doesn't minimize our sin. Consequently Jesus does indeed speak to this woman—and therefore speaks to us all—concerning what is wrong with us. However, by speaking his word of welcoming non-condemnation over this woman (who represents us all) *before* speaking to her of her sin, Jesus teaches us that it is not a person's sin that is the central and decisive fact concerning who they are or how God thinks about and behaves toward them. He teaches us that the first word he wants us to hear—and therefore the word that must shape the whole orientation of our lives and undergird our identity—is *not* about our sin, but rather about God's gracious word of welcoming non-condemnation toward us in and through Jesus Christ.

Notice also a second thing Jesus *doesn't* say. He doesn't say, "Go now and leave your life of sin and *then* I will not condemn you." The order is vitally important. So often we think God's order is that our turning away from sin must come *before* God's forgiveness—that God's acceptance of us is conditional upon and only comes as a result of our repentance and therefore that it is our faith and repentance that activates and causes us to receive God's mercy and forgiveness. But Jesus *first* assures this woman of his welcoming non-condemnation and *then*, as a consequence and in the context of this word of grace, he calls her to turn away from her life of sin. Jesus therefore teaches us that the first word he wants us to hear and accept (and therefore the first word we should speak to others and help them to hear and accept) is *not* about our (or their) sin—but rather, it is about God's gracious word of welcoming non-condemnation from out of which our repentance becomes the *consequence* of God's acceptance, rather than the *condition* by which it is obtained.

What this means is that Christian talk concerning sin must only take place from within the *context* of God's grace, by which sin is already named, exposed, and defeated in Jesus Christ and where all condemnation is already removed. Or as Voyle would express it, from out of a place that is life-giving and which orients people toward an open future in which they are empowered to reimagine and incarnate new ways of being and doing.

I believe we can discern the truth of this by simply asking, "How do we imagine Jesus intended this woman to engage in this demanding task of leaving her life of sin?" Do we imagine he intended this hard work of moral regeneration and transformation to take place for her as a solitary individual *outside of* the worshipping community and for her to gain entry only *after* she had accomplished this goal? Or are we to imagine he intended for her to engage in this task as *part of* a Jesus community? That is, as part of a community of faith that by the enabling power of God's Holy Spirit reminds itself daily that every one of us (regardless of how far along the path of moral regeneration we may or may not be) live daily only under the covering mercy of Jesus and his gracious word of welcoming non-condemnation. Surely we must understand Jesus to mean that this great work of moral regeneration is to take place *within* and therefore not *outside of* a Spirit-led community of faith.

As we saw in the previous chapter concerning faith; when we prioritize *behavior* over *relationship* we imperil so much. This is true also when we proclaim the Christian message in the wrong order, saying, "Go now and leave your life of sin and then God will not condemn you." When we do this we prioritize behavior over relationship and, in effect, tell people that they have to make themselves good enough (*behavior*) in order for God to accept them (*relationship*). Sadly many people believe this perverted gospel thinking it to be the message and invitation of Jesus. When this happens one of two terrible things usually follows. The first is they will try hard to make themselves good enough for God—*and think they have succeeded*. These people risk becoming moral Pharisees who are critical of those who obviously aren't trying hard enough to be as good as they are. They risk becoming spiritually arrogant, unmerciful, judgmental, and moralistic. The second is they will try hard to make themselves good enough for God—*and think they have failed*. If they are *honest* in their innermost thoughts these people risk becoming guilt-ridden and miserable—forever trying to be good enough for God, but always knowing they never will be. They risk becoming discouraged, defeated, and spiritually depressed. Alternatively, if they are *dishonest* in their innermost thoughts these people risk becoming hypocrites—pretending to others and to themselves that they really have made themselves good enough for God. They risk becoming inauthentic "plastic Christians" who sooner or later will be exposed as frauds.

4

Sin
—so what are we talking about?

As we have seen, God is a *relational* being who has created us as *relational beings* in order that we may enjoy *relationship* with God. This means that all the terms that describe the relationship God has with us must be understood *relationally*. We have already explored how this is true with regard to the key biblical concepts of "love" and "faith." The point I want to make in this chapter is that this is true also of "sin." This means we can really only understand this thing the Bible calls sin when we think about it primarily in *relational* terms—not in *behavioral* terms.

Despite the confidence with which Christian evangelistic tracts typically speak, the truth is that sin is actually very poorly understood by both Christians and non-Christians alike as simply being "bad things people do." This is a key reason Christian talk of sin is typically heard and received as bad news. However, when we gain a genuinely biblical understanding of "sin" this is profoundly liberating, life-giving, and life-changing. So let me say from the outset—the Christian doctrine of sin, rightly understood, is good news!

I believe there are at least three theological mistakes Christians typically make when thinking and speaking about sin. The first is that, in addressing people as sinners, we assume sin to be a normal aspect of human experience and consequently a category of thought that all people readily relate to and naturally understand. This was reinforced to me a while ago in quite a powerful way. I had been referred to some YouTube Christian mentoring videos in which someone explains Christian truths to new believers. Every time this person introduced a new theological concept like "grace," "forgiveness," or "salvation" he would carefully explain what these meant. What interested me is that he never did this with "sin"—he simply talked about it as though it was a self-evidently obvious human behavior that required no definition or explanation. However, the truth is that sin is *not* something we can self-evidently understand on the basis of our natural human knowledge and experience.

What we *can* know on this basis are: *crimes* like murder and rape; *atrocities* like war and terrorism; *psychological feelings* like guilt and shame; and *existential despair* like meaninglessness and hopelessness. But if we label these things "sin" we run into two problems. The first is that most people are more the victims of these things than perpetrators. Most people are in fact more "sinned against" than "sinners" if this is how we think about sin. Moreover, if the Christian evangelistic agenda at this point is to try and convince people that "all have sinned"—in other words that all are *perpetrators* of sin—then this can only sound like bad news. It risks re-victimizing and re-traumatizing those who have been sinned against by others all over again by making them responsible before God for the abusive actions of others.

The second problem is that modern society already has its own solutions to these things. Instead of "sin" and "salvation": sociologists talk of community dislocation and policies to curb criminal behavior; psychologists talk of emotional disintegration and better counseling techniques; educationalists talk of underachievement and better education programs; economists talk of poverty and better investment in infrastructure and job creation—and so on. Moreover, sensible Christians ought to agree that all these might be appropriate responses to different social issues in their proper contexts; but as a Christian understanding of sin all this is misdirected. As a description of our true condition in relation to God these things totally miss the point!

The second theological mistake is that when most Christians talk about sin what they mean is "bad things people do." But this is a *behavioral* rather than a *relational* way of thinking about sin. However, when we think relationally about this, we discover that sin is not primarily bad behavioral actions we do or attitudes we exhibit—rather, it is a dysfunctional relationship status we have. Sin is an alienated and dysfunctional relationship status we have with God that is evidenced by our bad attitudes and behaviors.

What this means is that our bad behavior is not the *cause* of our relationship with God being alienated and dysfunctional—rather it is the *confirmation* that it already is. Consequently our bad attitudes and behaviors are not the *cause* of our relationship with God being alienated and dysfunctional. Rather our bad behavior is the *symptom* that bears witness to the *disease*, not the disease itself.

Therefore, our bad behavior is the evidence and confirmation that our relationship with God is *already* alienated and dysfunctional. The truth is (even though in our natural state this knowledge is hidden from us) the thing that lies at the root of our bad behavior is the bewildered and anguished yearning of the alienated human heart that can only ever find its true end goal in relationship with God but, which apart from the grace of God, can only ever search for this end goal in misdirected and ultimately futile ways. Our bad behavior actually bears witness to the truth that, as Augustine says, "God has made us for himself and our hearts are restless until we find our rest in God." But outside of the grace of God it is impossible for us to see or understand this.

Treating symptoms is always bad medicine. It has been reported that the most common thing doctors do for homeless people is prescribe anti-depressants![1] However, a doctor who is any good—actually we should really say a doctor who is any good who is working within an overarching political, economic, social, and health system that is any good—uses the *symptom* to diagnose the *underlying problem* and then uses this knowledge to treat the *cause* of the underlying problem; and in this way restores the patient to full environmental, social, economic, physical, spiritual, and mental health such that the symptom no longer manifests. Or to put it another way—the reason we have symptoms, and why we should be grateful for them, is to alert us to the existence of the underlying problems that afflict us so that we will be motivated to get the help we need to treat the cause of the underlying problems we have!

Consequently, God doesn't cure the sin problem by commanding or pleading or threatening or bribing us to *behave better* (like so many desperate parents with their disobedient children do). If we think we can solve the sin problem by behaving better we either become guilt-ridden and miserable (if we think we fail), or smug and self-righteous (if we think we

1. Florence Kerr, "The Homeless Are Most Likely to Be Fed Anti-depressants When Reaching Out for Help, New Research Suggests," *Stuff*, July 13, 2020, www.stuff.co.nz/national/health/300054188/the-homeless-are-most-likely-to-be-fed-antidepressants-when-reaching-out-for-help-new-research-suggests.

succeed). Additionally, if we think God cures the sin problem by somehow getting us to behave better, all we do is perpetuate the deeply damaging religious myth that it is our behavior that determines our true being. However, God cures the sin problem, not by focusing on our *bad behavior*, but by establishing a *new relationship* with us. As we saw from Galatians 2:20 in chapter 3, God cures the sin problem by radical and unconventional surgery—by putting the old person of sin to death in Jesus Christ and then raising us up with him to new life in new relationship with God!

> I have been crucified with Christ and I no longer live, but Christ lives in me. The life I now live in the body, I live by faith in the Son of God, who loved me and gave himself for me.

Now, of course God does want us to behave better. But our doing so does not *cause* God to put our old person of sin to death in Jesus Christ and raise us to right relationship with him! The cause of our reconciled relationship with God is the gift of God's grace in Jesus Christ—something we can never cause to happen by our behavior. God wants us to live a life that corresponds to and aligns with his loving mercy for three reasons: first, this bears confirming witness to the authenticity of the new relationship we have with God; second, living in conformity with God's covenantal love is God's way of enlarging our capacity to receive and give love; and third, God knows this will help make us happier people. But none of this good behavior is the cause of our reconciled relationship with God. The cause of our reconciled relationship with God is the gift of God's grace in Jesus Christ that comes to us out of the covenantal *chesed* faithfulness of God made real in our lives by the enabling power of God's Holy Spirit.

The truth is that we can only know about our true condition—our dysfunctional and alienated relationship with God—by the grace of God. Therefore, a true understanding of our sin problem is only revealed to us as we understand what God has done to reconcile and redeem us in Jesus Christ. As we saw in the previous chapter from the woman accused of adultery in John 8, we can really only come to know this in a healthy way as part of a Jesus community that affirms and celebrates God's gracious word of welcoming non-condemnation that God speaks over each one of us in and through Jesus Christ.

The knowledge concerning our alienated and dysfunctional relationship with God is only disclosed to us as we receive and reflect on the mercy and love of God through which we come to an understanding that our sin has *already* been defeated in Jesus Christ. The great old hymn "Amazing

Grace" expresses good theology when it says, "'Twas grace that taught my heart to fear and grace my fears relieved." Outside of the grace of God revealed to us in Jesus Christ we simply cannot understand ourselves to be sinners, alienated from God, and living in contradiction to who and what God has created us to be. Moreover, the fact that we cannot in our natural selves understand this is actually part of our sin problem!

In our natural selves, outside of the grace of God, we simply have no categories of thought within which to properly understand our true condition, for it is only in the *cure* that the *disease* is understood. Outside of the grace of God all we confront is a series of misdiagnoses, false cures, and false hopes. Therefore the true knowledge of our condition, as this is disclosed to us in Jesus Christ, ought to be greeted with enormous relief and rejoicing. Christian talk about sin ought to be good news, not bad news. It ought to be talk of the malaise that afflicts us, our release from its bondage, and our acceptance by God, who has already defeated our sin in Jesus Christ—not talk of our condemnation and shame.

This is like someone who has suffered long from a baffling illness that no doctor has recognized or understood and who has only been given pain relief to alleviate their symptoms (like a deeply unhappy homeless person desperately seeking help who is simply given anti-depressants) or else dismissed as being a delusional hypochondriac. However, they have now discovered that the most eminent doctor of all not only recognizes their disease, but has named it and made it their life's work to provide a cure that is now in place. Knowing this can only produce relief and rejoicing. It means we are not simply imagining our symptoms—that we not delusional hypochondriacs. Rather it means that the baffling malaise that has dogged our every step is actually real and has a name. But, most importantly, the condition has been recognized and addressed by God himself and so all our futile efforts at self-diagnosis and self-medication can finally be dispensed with—Hallelujah!

The third theological mistake Christians so often make is assuming that the sin problem is primarily *our* fault and *our* responsibility. In Genesis 4 we encounter the first use of the word "sin" in the Bible. Cain and Abel both offer gifts, but for some unexplained reason:

> The Lord had regard for Abel and his offering, but for Cain and his offering he had no regard.

In response to this we read, "Cain was very angry, and his countenance fell." Then in 4:6–7:

> The Lord said to Cain, "Why are you angry? Why is your face downcast? If you do what is right, will you not be accepted? But if you do not do what is right, sin is crouching at your door; it desires to have you, but you must rule over it.

What is so important to understand here is that in describing sin as "*crouching* at your door" and that "it *desires* to have you" the Bible is clearly not describing sin as bad behavioral actions *we* do. This is the same in Romans 7:8–11, where Paul says:

> But sin, seizing the opportunity afforded by the commandment, produced in me every kind of coveting. For apart from the law, sin was dead. Once I was alive apart from the law; but when the commandment came, sin sprang to life and I died. I found that the very commandment that was intended to bring life actually brought death. For sin, seizing the opportunity afforded by the commandment, deceived me, and through the commandment put me to death.

Notice how Paul describes sin here—he describes it as *seizing* an opportunity, *producing in him* covetous desires, experiencing a resurrection-like *springing to life, deceiving* him, and then *putting him to death*. These are clearly all behavioral actions, but not actions that Paul himself does! Rather, they are the behavioral actions of some external agent that does these things *to* Paul. But if we simply think of sin as "bad things *we* do" then the way the Bible speaks of sin here makes no sense whatsoever. This is because in these passages sin is spoken of not as evil things *we* do, but as some kind of spiritual power or demonic force that does evil things *to us*!

In this part of Romans Paul doesn't speak of sin as our behavior at all. Instead, he speaks of it as a kind of scheming opportunist and cunning predator that conceals itself, "crouching at the door," as it were, waiting for the chance to pounce. Its tactic being to deceive us by using God's good and holy commandment and our sincere desire to try and obey it as a kind of bait to lure us into its trap—and then to kill and devour us. As Paul reflects on the way this evil power produces all manner of covetousness within him—things that are in contradiction to both his true desire and best interest—he says in 7:20:

Sin—So What Are We Talking About?

> Now if I do what I do not want to do, it is no longer I who do it, but it is sin living in me that does it.

This is very strange and disturbing language:

> *If I do what I do not want to do . . .*

What we must remember, as we saw in the previous chapter, is that Paul is referring here to two different *I*'s. Moreover, it is actually very common for people to speak of themselves in this deeply disturbing disconnected-from-their-true-self way—yet remain unaware of the profoundly important truth this feeling of inner alienation points to. For example, it is not uncommon to hear people say, "I hate myself."

Again there are two different *I*'s here. The first is *myself* who is hated, blamed, and shamed by another being who *myself* thoughtlessly calls *I*—a being who hates and despises the true *myself*—an evil being who masquerades as the real me but who, in truth, is an imposter whose true identity remains concealed. It is precisely because this being remains concealed and unrecognized that it can therefore take something good and holy, like the law of God and my sincere Christian desire to try and obey it, and then use it to inflict all manner of guilt and shame upon me until in dutiful obedience to its relentless toxic logic not only does *I* hate myself, but *myself* learns to hate myself as well.

Now sometimes people try to excuse themselves, saying, "The devil made me do it," and of course most people, including Christians, are reluctant to give this idea any sort of credibility. This is because it has been ingrained in us that sin is something that we (alone) do and therefore something we (alone) must take responsibility for—and of course this is true. But in light of what God reveals to us in the gospel of Jesus Christ it is only true to a point. Because at one level the person who says, "The devil made me do it" is right! Listen again to what Paul is saying:

> Now if I do what I do not want to do, it is no longer I who do it, but it is sin living in me that does it.

In this way not only does Paul describe sin as an evil, scheming opportunist and a cunning malign predator, he also describes it as a thinking, acting, demonic being that infiltrates our desires and functioning and causes us to think and behave in ways that are in contradiction to how our true *I* genuinely wants to live and act. In other words, in ways that are in contradiction to how we truly *want* to live and act when we are in our right minds—which of course, because of sin, we aren't!

Consider all the self-destructive, self-sabotaging, utterly mad, highly addictive and dysfunctional ways in which we so often think and act and live! What Paul says here actually begins to make a lot of sense concerning the true nature of our human existence and the true nature of the evil that confronts us—that we humans *aren't* in our right minds. The truth is that at a profoundly deep and disturbing level we are infected by a malicious alien influence by which, perversely, we hate and act against our true selves—the true self that God has created each one of us to be in Jesus Christ.

A helpful way to get our heads around this is to distinguish between "Sin" and "sins." First we need to understand "Sin" as this hostile demonic force that has invaded us—this evil being that seeks our destruction and which, through the gospel of Jesus Christ, God has named, defeated, and exposed for what it truly is. What this means is that when we speak of "Sin" we must be clear that it is this evil force or being we are speaking of and not people's bad behavior. Second we need to understand "sins" as the behavioral actions we do as a symptomatic secondary consequence on account of the influence of this demonic force that operates within us—that is, the bad behaviors that this demonic being stirs up within us to want to do as the *symptoms* manifested by us that bear witness to the *disease* we are infected by.

What this means is that we are actually caught up in something that is much bigger than just *our* bad behavior. In other words, "Sin" is much bigger than just our "sins." Nevertheless it also means that none of us are entirely *innocent* victims in this whole business because we also, at one level or another, are *willing* victims. The truth is, at one level or another, we welcome this malign influence, delight in the desires it stirs up within us, and like so many drug addicts, instinctively resist the cure God provides.

Much of this is a mystery. Nevertheless, Holy Scripture requires us to simultaneously affirm the following two (seemingly contradictory) opposites and hold them together. First, God calls us to take responsibility for our bad behavior because of the fact that we willingly and knowingly do "sins." But also, second, we are caught up in a conflict that is much bigger than ourselves that we are not responsible for on account of the evil that is external to us but which operates within us—this thing we must recognize as "Sin."

Moreover, we must also understand that the evil that confronts us is not primarily opposed to us. The truth of the matter is that the evil that confronts us is only *secondarily* opposed to us on account of the fact that it is *primarily* opposed to God—and therefore only wants to hurt and destroy us because we are the subjects of God's love. This then is the strange (and also strangely *comforting*) thing about this whole "Sin" and "sins" business—the underlying reason we humans here on earth have become caught up in this is because we are the subjects of God's covenantal *chesed* love! In a strange way this is actually very encouraging—we have only *secondarily* become the objects of this evil being's malicious attention because *primarily* we are the subjects of God's love—and because this evil being hates what God loves. What this means is that if God didn't love us "Sin" would leave us alone. If God didn't regard us as his much loved sons and daughters then this evil being wouldn't concern itself with us. Consequently we are kind of "civilian casualties" in someone else's war. We are a sort of "collateral damage" on account of our being caught up in a more primary and fundamental conflict between powerful others that doesn't directly involve us.

We actually get a glimpse of this in the lurid imagery of Revelation 12:13–17:

> When the dragon saw that he had been hurled to the earth, he pursued the woman who had given birth to the male child. The woman was given the two wings of a great eagle, so that she might fly to the place prepared for her in the wilderness, where she would be taken care of for a time, times and half a time, out of the serpent's reach. Then from his mouth the serpent spewed water like a river, to overtake the woman and sweep her away with the torrent. But the earth helped the woman by opening its mouth and swallowing the river that the dragon had spewed out of his mouth. Then the dragon was enraged at the woman and went off to wage war against the rest of her offspring—those who keep God's commands and hold fast their testimony about Jesus.

What this means is that because the dragon couldn't get at the one who gave birth to the male child (God in heaven, its primary target) it instead wages war upon the offspring of the one who gave birth to the male child (us here on earth, its secondary target). Consequently, the very fact that we are caught up in this whole business and are therefore tormented by sinful desire aroused by the dragon (in the way Paul describes this in Romans 7) is compelling evidence that we are loved by God and care deeply about the new relationship we have with God through Jesus Christ. Moreover, it is evidence that this evil influence knows that it has been "hurled to the earth" and therefore already mastered by God, exposed for what it truly is, and its fraudulent claim upon us defeated in Jesus Christ!

5

Christ Died for Our Sins
—so what has God done and for whom?

IN THE LAST TWO chapters we have worked with Galatians 2:20—the Apostle Paul saying:

> I have been crucified with Christ and I no longer live, but Christ lives in me.

The question I now want to ask in relation to this is, "*When* precisely did the crucifixion of the old Paul of sin take place with Christ?" There are two possible answers. One is that it took place the moment he personally became aware of Christ's death on his behalf and chose to embrace this as a reality in his own life through faith. In other words, it happened in a set of circumstances unique to Paul himself—namely, on the road to Damascus (or perhaps shortly thereafter at his baptism at a certain address on Straight Street) in an event we would call his *conversion* that he would subsequently speak of in what we would call his *testimony*.

The other possible answer is that the crucifixion of the old Paul of sin took place the very same moment Jesus himself was crucified—namely, on a Roman cross on a hill just outside of Jerusalem on the first Easter around 33 AD. In other words, the crucifixion of the old Paul of sin happened in a set of circumstances completely outside of and removed from the specifics of his own life in an event that is universally identical for all humanity that Paul would subsequently speak of as *the good news of Christ crucified*.

Consequently, when *we* are asked, "When were *you* saved?" what answer do we give? When we are asked, "When did God reconcile *you* to himself?" "When did God elect to no longer count *your* sins against you?" "When was the precise moment God broke down, demolished, and obliterated the barrier that kept *you* separated from God?" how do we answer? The thing that is so important we understand is that the way we answer this question decisively shapes two things—the way we regard others, and the nature of the message we proclaim.

From what many Christians typically say it very much seems they believe God's reconciling, saving mercy comes into existence for specific individuals at the moment of their conversion. The clear implication therefore is that for any particular person, prior to this moment of awareness and response, their status with God was such that God had not (yet) reconciled them to himself; not (yet) elected to no longer count their sins against them; and not (yet) broken down the barrier of separation that had kept them alienated from God. This implies therefore that in our pre-conversion condition of unbelief God had erected a barrier against us that he has not (yet) removed for us personally. Consequently the good news of Jesus is thought to be about how God is willing to open a door through this barrier to allow certain individuals who profess faith to come through—and then bolts the door shut again against everyone else who doesn't!

Now if this really is the way it is then this means we must picture God's reconciling action in the event of the cross of Christ as a kind of *potential* salvation that is dependent upon a specific person's response in order to become effective in the life of that person. We must picture it therefore as a kind of infinite entry in God's heavenly ledger against the sins of the world that God only draws down, credits to, and activates for specific people *individually* on a case by case basis at the moment of their conversion. What this means is that up until this moment each person exists in a state of alienation from God's saving work—our status with God having hitherto remained unaffected and unchanged by what God did that day on the cross when Jesus cried, "It is finished," and the curtain in the temple was torn in two from top to bottom.

It is certainly true that there are many Bible passages that can be read in support of this view. For example, in Acts 2:38 Peter urges his listeners to repent and save themselves from their wicked generation by believing in Jesus and being baptized. This certainly gives the impression that if they *don't* then they *won't*. However, the Bible also teaches that the saving work of

Jesus has changed the situation of *all people* irrespective of whether or not they have personally appropriated this truth to themselves through faith.[1] The reason we can say this is because, in his sovereign will, God is pleased at key moments to regard the actions of a *representative one* as impacting upon and changing the situation of a *collective whole*—and in this way attributing to the collective whole all that the representative one has done on their behalf. We see this especially in relation to Adam and Jesus. For example, we read in Romans 5:18:

> Consequently, just as one trespass [by Adam in the garden] resulted in condemnation for all people, so also one righteous act [by Jesus on the cross] resulted in justification and life for all people.

Also 1 Corinthians 15:21:

> For since death came through a man, the resurrection of the dead comes also through a man. For as in Adam all die, so in Christ all will be made alive.

In light of this it is instructive to consider in some detail what Paul says in 2 Corinthians 5 concerning this curious way in which God deems the behavior of a representative one (Jesus) to impact upon and change the situation of a collective whole (all humanity). In 5:14 he says:

> For Christ's love compels us, because we are convinced that one died for all, and therefore all died.

Paul is convinced that when Jesus died on the cross he died for *all humanity* and therefore in this mysterious representative "one for all" way at that very moment, in the reckoning of God, all humanity was gathered up and included in this event—and therefore *all died*. What this means is that God has elected to regard the experience of Jesus on the cross as gathering up, impacting upon, and thus changing the status of all humanity. Indeed, as Paul reflects on this in Colossians 1:19–20, he understands the scope of God's saving work in Jesus Christ to embrace not just *all humanity*—but *all creation*!

> For God was pleased to have all his fullness dwell in [Christ] and through him to reconcile to himself all things, whether things on earth or things in heaven, by making peace through his blood, shed on the cross.

---

1. For further discussion around this question, see Parry and Partridge, *Universal Salvation?*

What happened to Jesus as our *representative one* on the cross God deems to have impacted upon and changed the situation of *every person*—irrespective of how any *specific person* may or may not (yet) have personally responded to this. Therefore, it is entirely possible for the true *status* of the relationship that any particular person has with God to be very different to what they *think* it is or how this person actually *experiences* this relationship. This is because it is entirely possible for specific individuals to be ignorant of or unaccepting of their true relationship status with God and therefore not enter into and participate in this relationship as a lived experiential reality.

Let me illustrate. A while ago I heard about a man who had become alienated from his family. He felt they didn't value him because he thought they viewed him as an embarrassing failure and so in his humiliation he drifted away, stopped communicating, and over many years they lost contact. However, as an older man he learned he didn't have long to live and yearned to reconnect. What he discovered was that for all these years they had all lived with a misunderstanding. The truth was that his family hadn't rejected him at all, but thought he had died, and they were now filled with joy to discover he was still alive and wanted very much to reconnect.

This man *thought* or *believed* that the true status of his relationship with his family was that they had rejected him. However, from their side the truth was that they loved him, but thought he was dead. Consequently, because of this misunderstanding or misbelief, they were prevented as a family from enjoying the true status of their relationship as an experiential lived reality. What a tragedy! What a waste! All those years, both believing something about the true status of the relationship between them that was false—and this false belief robbing them of the blessing of enjoying the true status of their relationship as a daily lived experience.

We see this same thing in the story of the prodigal son in Luke 15. The young son has behaved badly toward his family, experienced the shame that so often follows such behavior, and consequently alienated himself from what he believes is the source of his shame. Later on though, a bit like the man in my story, the son decides to reconnect. He is convinced that the true status of his relationship with his family is that they have rejected him as a son and brother. His great hope, however, is that they might give him a job as a servant. Nevertheless, the true status of the relationship from the father's side is that he loves him as his son. In fact, he has never stopped loving his son and has long since forgiven every offense. The father yearns in hope for his son's return so that they can participate together again as a family in the daily blessing of enjoying the true status of their relationship as an experiential lived reality. The father's great hope for his son (for *both* his sons actually) is that they will accept their relationship status with him and as a consequence learn to behave in ways that are consistent with their true status as their father's sons and therefore brothers of each other.

Now, flowing out of the fact that in Jesus Christ "one died for all and therefore all died," Paul in the remainder of 2 Corinthians 5 makes two key points. The first is that if we genuinely understand and take to heart that through Jesus Christ God has reconciled all people to himself—even though not all people necessarily understand, accept, respond to, or live consistently according to their true relationship status with God (yet)—this shapes the way we Christians are to now regard and behave toward all people. He goes on to say in 5:15–17:

> And he died for all, that those who live should no longer live for themselves but for him who died for them and was raised again. So from now on we regard no one from a worldly point of view. Though we once regarded Christ in this way, we do so no longer. Therefore, if anyone is in Christ, the new creation has come; the old has gone, the new is here!

Unfortunately Paul's attempt to make his thought clear is frustrated at this point given that many Bibles mistranslate this passage, saying:

> Therefore, if anyone is in Christ, he is a new creation; the old has gone, the new has come!

But the words "he is a" are absent in the Greek. What Paul actually says is:

> Therefore, if anyone is in Christ, new creation; the old has gone, the new has come!

However, by inserting the words "he is a" this has the effect of *individualizing* the reconciling work of God and reinforcing the impression that God's salvation is something that only comes into existence individually to specific people on a case-by-case basis at the moment of their conversion.

Paul's point however is that if there is *anyone* in Christ—*anyone at all*—then this means that God's new creation has broken into history and impacted upon *all* creation and as a result changed the status of *all* humanity. Therefore, the fact that there are *some* in Christ—that is, the fact that by the life-giving work of God's Holy Spirit there is a community of Christian witness in the world—this is evidence that the old has gone, the new has come. It means that as far as God is concerned we can know with assurance that *all* have died and therefore there is now no one whom God counts their sin against. Consequently, because this new reality has changed the status of every person in *God's* reckoning, this means *we* need to change *our* reckoning in terms of how we regard and behave toward others as well—"So from now on we regard no one from a worldly point of view."

What this means is that in light of what God has wrought for every individual in Jesus Christ, from now on we must no longer live by the old, elitist, discriminatory rules that accord grace to just a historically privileged subgroup of humanity. From now on we are to understand that God's reconciling mercy in Jesus Christ embraces and includes *all people*—regardless of their religious pedigree, past, spiritual condition, moral status, or economic and social circumstances—regardless of their race, culture, class origins, gender, sexual orientation, or anything else external or accidental about them! In light of the fact that God's saving work in Jesus Christ embraces *all* humanity, Paul's first key point is therefore "from now on we regard no one from a worldly point of view."

In this way, what God has done in Jesus Christ—"reconciling to himself all things, whether things on earth or things in heaven, by making peace through his blood, shed on the cross"—has the same force as God declaring through Jeremiah the prophet in 31:33:

> I will be their God and they will be my people.

As we emphasized in chapter 1; every covenant God establishes with his human creatures is always at God's initiative, always on God's terms, and always an expression of God's desire to bring people into loving relationship with himself—the God who *is* love. God has determined to be our God and for us to be his people—*whether we like it or not*! From the point of view of God's sovereign decision in *chesed* faithfulness to reconcile the world to himself through Jesus Christ—any particular person's *liking* or *accepting* or *approving* or *agreeing with* God's decision is of no consequence. Our believing and accepting (or else *not* believing and *not* accepting) does not change the objective reality of what God has done in the event of the cross one iota. Our individual response to this reality simply determines how we will personally *enjoy* (or perhaps *not* enjoy) the fact that God has elected to be our God and for us to be his people.

Paul's second key point is that not only does "one died for all and therefore all died" determine the way God calls us to *regard* all others, it also determines *the message we proclaim*. He continues in 5:18–20 saying:

> All this is from God, who reconciled us to himself through Christ and gave us the ministry of reconciliation: that God was reconciling the world to himself in Christ, not counting people's sins against them. And he has committed to us the message of reconciliation. We are therefore Christ's ambassadors, as though God were making his appeal through us. We implore you on Christ's behalf: Be reconciled to God.

Paul then concludes in v. 21 with another representative "one for all" statement that echoes, expands upon, and sums up the one he began with:

> God made him who had no sin to be sin for us, so that in him we might become the righteousness of God.

The primary theological fact that "God was reconciling the world to himself in Christ, not counting people's sins against them" therefore determines the nature of the ministry God has given to us as Christ's ambassadors to proclaim to every person, "We implore you on Christ's behalf: Be reconciled to God!" On account of the fact that God has *already* reconciled all humanity to himself in Christ, all people are therefore called individually to consciously respond to this with their own personal decision to be reconciled to God. Furthermore, the people God calls to proclaim this message and do this imploring are those who already know and have experienced this truth—those who have already consciously been reconciled to God!

The Bible therefore points to two decisive moments concerning God's salvation in which our relationship status with God is radically changed. The first moment is when *God reconciled us to himself* in Christ on the cross just outside of Jerusalem on the first Easter around 33 AD—that salvation moment that irrevocably changed the true relationship status of every person with God and which is universally identical for each individual and which embraces all humanity. The second moment is the event in which *we are reconciled to God* through faith at the moment of our conversion—that salvation moment that is unique to each particular person in which specific individuals become consciously aware of and enabled to participate in their true relationship status with God as a daily lived experience.

The first decisive moment establishes and determines the objective reality of our true relationship status with God. It is the moment God brought into existence for all humanity and all creation once and for all when God reconciled the world to himself through Jesus Christ on the cross—the event through which God elected to no longer count our sins against us, thus establishing peace. This was an *objective* (and therefore *outside of us*) event through which God established the true relationship status with every person long before any particular person came into existence or to awareness—a relationship status of reconciliation and peace that originated from out of the covenantal *chesed* faithfulness of God which has been declared by the verdict of God in the gospel of Christ whether we (yet) know and accept this or not!

The second decisive moment establishes and determines our subjective conscious participation in the true relationship status every person has with God. It is the moment when God makes this new relationship status an experiential lived relational reality in the lives of specific individuals personally on a case by case basis. It happens when God, by his Holy Spirit, enables us to be consciously reconciled to God at the moment of our conversion through which God pours his peace into our hearts through faith. This is a *subjective* (and therefore *within us*) relational experience we have with God that is true for us personally that originates from out of the covenantal *chesed* faithfulness of God, which enables us to accept and consciously participate in relationship with God through the Holy Spirit by faith.

It is important we understand that *both* of these salvation moments— (1) God reconciling the world to himself through Christ on the cross; and (2) our being reconciled to God individually through faith in Jesus at the moment of our conversion—need to be *held together* yet also *distinguished from* one another.

Two theological mistakes are commonly made at this point. The first is to fail to hold these two salvation moments in proper distinction and separation and therefore to merge them together and thus regard them as one and the same thing. This mistake arises when we think that God's salvation becomes an actual reality only at the moment of a person's conversion experience—that is, when we think that a person's conversion experience is the precise moment God reconciles them to himself; elects to no longer count their sins against them; and breaks down, demolishes, and obliterates the barrier that has kept them separated from God. When we think in these terms the tendency is to slide into an individualistic understanding of God's salvation in which the believer's primary focus is on "me and my personal relationship with God" without reference to God's wider concern for all humanity and all creation.

The second mistake is to fail to hold these two salvation moments together in proper unity and oneness and therefore to separate them and regard them as two entirely disconnected events. This mistake arises when we think that God's salvation in Jesus Christ is something that happened in the ancient past—something that happened in some historically truthful way on the cross, but unrelated to our personal lives in the here and now. When we think in these terms the tendency is to slide into a mere intellectual acknowledgment of the truth of God. It risks giving rise to a formalistic expression of Christian faith, devoid of a vibrant living heart-level relationship with God.

However, as we have emphasized, because God is a *relational* god who has created us as God's human creatures for *relationship*, this means that all the key terms that describe this relationship need to be primarily understood *relationally*. But in our natural human condition we struggle to think relationally and therefore tend to emphasize contract over covenant when we think about "love," doctrinal content over relationship when we think about "faith," and behavior over relationship when we think about "sin." In the same way when we think about "salvation" the Christian tendency is to think primarily in terms of place or circumstance rather than relationship. In other words, there is a widespread Christian tendency to think that the key thing this whole business boils down to is that we end up in the right *place* or *circumstance* when we die—about what we are saved *from* rather than saved *to* and *for*. But thinking this way completely bypasses the fact that God's overriding concern is *relational* and therefore we find our true joy in the fullness of our true humanity only in right relationship with God—and then flowing out of this in right relationship with ourselves, others, and the world.

I believe C. S. Lewis in *The Chronicles of Narnia*[2] demonstrates this key insight that the salvation we have in God is primarily about *relationship* rather than *place* or *circumstance*. He pictures the dwarves, who have for so long refused to put their trust in Aslan because they refuse to be "taken in," as being in the new eschatological Narnia (the *place* that God has prepared for his creatures to be *saved to*)—but they are unable to recognize this fact. The dwarves are in paradise, but believe themselves to be in a dark stinking stable. Eustace and Jill plead with Aslan to help the dwarves understand

---

2. Lewis, *Chronicles of Narnia*, 746.

their true relationship status and condition to which he replies, "Dearest... I will show you both what I can and cannot do." He speaks to the dwarves, but they think it is a trick; he gives them a banquet, but they think it is stable food—and then each suspects the others have something better and they begin to fight. But after nursing their wounds they console themselves saying, "Well at any rate there is no humbug here. We haven't let anyone take us in." Aslan then explains to the children:

> You see... they will not let us help them. They have chosen cunning instead of belief. Their prison is only in their own minds, yet they are in that prison; and so afraid of being taken in that they cannot be taken out.

Yet again the nearest analogy we have to understanding the distinction between our true *objective* relationship status we have in God through Christ and our *subjective* participation in this objective relationship status through faith is the relationship we have with our children. Our children don't come into the world behind a bolted door we have erected that separates them from our love. Nor is their great task to find and win our love by making themselves attractive or good enough for us to open our door to them. Rather they come into the world *already* surrounded by our love and their great task (and ours also) is that, as they grow and develop, they become aware of, learn to trust as true, and enter into the love that already surrounds them in real and genuinely relational ways.

So it is with God. The good news of Jesus Christ is that on the cross, God has obliterated and destroyed all barriers and bolted doors against relationship with Godself. Therefore any barriers that remain are ones that we have erected from our side against God. But from God's side, God wants us to know that we are *already* enfolded within God's eternal, reconciling loving-kindness—and that this is true whether we know and accept this or not. Our great task therefore is not to try and *find love*, but to awaken to the reality that *love has already found us*—and that God invites all humanity, and each individual specifically, to participate in this love in conscious and experiential ways with God, with each other, and with all creation *here and now*. This is the ministry of reconciliation that God has called us as ambassadors of Christ to share with others—imploring all people on Christ's behalf, "Be reconciled to God" because "God has [*already*] reconciled you to himself."

So the great question we face concerning our standing with God is not whether God will accept us—but whether we will accept the fact that in

Jesus Christ God has *already* accepted us. The great question we encounter concerning our present existence is not whether God will reconcile us into right relationship so that we may enjoy God's blessing—but whether we will enter into God's blessing as an enjoyed present reality because God has *already* reconciled us into right relationship with himself. And the great question we confront concerning our ultimate fate and destiny is not whether God, because of our unbelief, will judge us unworthy of eternal life and therefore consign us to an eternity of being separated from God—but whether we, because of our unbelief (like the dwarves) will judge God unworthy of us and therefore consign ourselves to an eternity of our rejecting God.

But what about the three kinds of individualism we need to guard ourselves against from chapter 1? Is the fate of the dwarves who are so terrified of being taken in (because their trust has previously been so terribly abused) really to spend all eternity in Aslan's paradise believing it to be a dark stinking stable? And what of the happiness of the children—can they truly be expected to spend all eternity in Aslan's paradise knowing the miserable fate of the dwarves they care so deeply about?

As C. S. Lewis tells the story, Eustace "had no time to wonder about [those he had known who were either included or excluded from life in the new eschatological Narnia] . . . for a great joy put everything else out of his head."[3] This being so then presumably the dwarves are to forever remain squabbling in what they imagine is a dark stinking stable—learning nothing concerning their true status and location. And presumably the children are to forever remain blissfully unaware of this fact and therefore never saddened by the thought of the miserable condition of the dwarves on account of the great joy that Aslan has overwhelmed them with. Hardly a satisfactory conclusion I would suggest!

From what I understand of the children, as C. S. Lewis tells the story, I simply cannot imagine them being happy with this outcome. As I understand Eustace and Jill—and certainly as I understand Lucy—their innate sense of love and justice and goodness would implore of Aslan that he try harder to help the dwarves to see, understand, and accept their true status and condition—and not just to give up after his first failed effort. Failing this I can easily imagine them imploring of Aslan that *they* be permitted to try and reason with the dwarves themselves; to love them with a view to winning their trust so as to overcome their fear of being taken in so

---

3. Lewis, *Chronicles of Narnia*, 751.

that they can (eventually) be taken out—and to stay there with them until they have succeeded! Moreover I can imagine how angry and disappointed the children would be if they ever discovered that the great joy Aslan has overwhelmed them with had actually caused them to *forget* the people they all care deeply about.

The truth is that any person's joy in the new eschatological Narnia can only be made genuinely full if it includes the restoration to wholeness of *all* the people and living creatures this person cares deeply about. Therefore, for Aslan to *genuinely* care deeply for Eustace and Jill and Lucy as persons who have been formed in relationship with others (including the dwarves), then he must also care deeply about all the people and living creatures in their networks of relationships they care about (including the dwarves). But for Aslan to genuinely care deeply about all the people in *their* networks of relationships, then he must also care deeply about all those more distant others in the many networks of these others—and so on in an unbroken chain of human and living creature connection from the present moment of every person who has ever lived down to the dawn of creation.

But of course for us to imagine that Eustace or Jill or Lucy or Tirian or Peter or Susan or Edmund's innate sense of love and justice and goodness is somehow greater than Aslan's is to make an utter nonsense out of who it is that C. S. Lewis is trying to portray Aslan as being in this wonderful allegory of Jesus Christ. The Apostle Paul speaks of these things in 1 Corinthians 15—the resurrection of Christ and God's new creation. In 15:22–28 he says:

> For as in Adam all die, so in Christ all will be made alive. But each in turn: Christ, the firstfruits; then, when he comes, those who belong to him. Then the end will come, when he hands over the kingdom to God the Father after he has destroyed all dominion, authority and power. For he must reign until he has put all his enemies under his feet. The last enemy to be destroyed is death. For he "has put everything under his feet." Now when it says that "everything" has been put under him, it is clear that this does not include God himself, who put everything under Christ. When he has done this, then the Son himself will be made subject to him who put everything under him, so that God may be all in all.

The Christian vision of the fulfillment of all things is that when all opposition to the love and justice and goodness of God has finally been overcome then "God [will] be all in all"—the fullness of God filling all creation and all humanity. But so long as the dwarves remain in their self-created prison, and so long as the children require Aslan's great joy of forgetfulness to keep them from this awareness that would otherwise greatly sadden them, we cannot yet say that "God is all in all."

6

God's Perfect World
—so what went wrong?

As I emphasized in the introduction this is an appreciative inquiry into Christian talk about sin and salvation. As we have seen, the key idea in appreciative inquiry is not to focus primarily on what is *wrong* with people—which almost always results in shame, and all the dysfunctional and destructive behaviors that flow out of shame—but to affirm what is working and life-giving. For me, as a Christian minister and theologian, this means rethinking the language and underlying presuppositions we have traditionally employed to speak of God's relationship with us—*in light of Jesus Christ*. Yet as we saw in chapter 3, Christian evangelistic proclamation so often focuses on what is wrong with people by addressing them as "sinners." Now the key theological presupposition that so often lies at the root of typical Christian evangelistic proclamation is the (supposed) fact of God's "perfection" as the standard against which our sin must be understood.

Two Christian tracts have recently come through my letter box. The first (and worst) asks, "How is your relationship with God?" and then immediately says:

> God is Holy: Romans 3:23 "For all have sinned and come short of the glory of God." God cannot tolerate our sin. He must punish it. Due to his holy nature, God's standard is perfection.[1]

---

1. See www.lighthouseindependentbaptistchurch.com.

The second is the *Hope Project*—the most well-resourced evangelistic effort in New Zealand this generation. It does a much better job of making connection, but the underlying theology is the same. They say:

> Even if we try we cannot be perfect. [And this is] a problem . . . to our Creator because he is *perfect*.[2]

These tracts go on to speak of God being loving and gracious, but notice the emphasis—everything revolves around God being "perfect" and the great problem this creates on account of our human "imperfection."

The idea that God is perfect, and therefore the standard he requires of us is perfection, traces its origins to the opening chapters of Genesis and the widespread Christian idea that in the garden of Eden God had created a perfect world modeled on God's heavenly template. As we survey the history of Christian thought, this idea gained traction from around the mid-second century as Christian thinking was influenced—and as time went on, *deeply* influenced—by Platonic Greek philosophy. What this means therefore is that this idea concerning the perfection of Eden doesn't actually come *from* the Bible; but from a Christianized version of Platonic philosophy that has been *read back into* the Bible.[3] Plato believed the world is always changing and therefore cannot be trusted to reveal the underlying truth of reality. For Plato, permanence and certainty, and therefore eternity and truth—and therefore *perfection*—is only found in some transcendent other-worldly realm. And from the second century most Christians were happy to identify this unchanging (Platonic) "perfection" with God in heaven.

Christians therefore began to describe God as *immutable* and *impassible*. Immutable means "never changing"—the logic being that anyone who changes cannot be perfect. If you change you must either have moved toward perfection or away from it. Either way you must have once been, or now are, imperfect. Impassible means "unable to suffer"—the logic being that those who suffer undergo change and therefore cannot be perfect.

---

2. *Hope for All* (Hope Project tract, 2014), 23, emphasis original; see https://alltogether.co.nz/hopeproject2014/.

3. In much of what follows in this chapter and the next I am working with two key ideas from McLaren, *A New Kind of Christianity*. The first is the way Christian faith has been deeply influenced by Platonic philosophy, especially how this has come to be expressed in what McLaren calls the "six-line model"; and the second, that the Bible invites us into a much more imaginative reading of the early chapters of Genesis than traditional Christian orthodoxy has generally been willing to allow.

In John 1:18 we read:

> No one has ever seen God, but the one and only Son, who is himself God and is in closest relationship with the Father, has made him known.

This means that our understanding of God must come—not from Plato, and not from Platonized Christians either—but from Jesus Christ. When we look to Jesus, what we see is that the two key moments in his life we celebrate as Christmas and Easter—"The Word became flesh and dwelt among us" represents a great *change* in God; and Jesus crying out from the cross, "My God my God why have you forsaken me?" represents great *suffering* in God.

Yet despite what we see so clearly in Jesus, this idea concerning the immutable and impassible perfection of God has hung on for so long in Christian thinking to the extent that it has become the standard lens through which so many Christians read the Bible. As a result the standard reading of Genesis chapters 1 and 2 is about how God created the eternal perfection of heaven—*on earth*. And Genesis chapter 3 onward about how imperfect humans caused a cosmic catastrophe that has forever set God's creation on a collision course with hell; and God's plan to restore his original state of perfection back in its proper place—*in heaven*.

However, as I say, this idea doesn't come *from* the Bible; but from a Christianized version of Platonic philosophy that has been read back into the Bible. Therefore Christian evangelistic proclamation that begins with the presupposition that God's standard is "perfection" is the result of pasting a Christianized Platonic ideal onto God; pasting this onto God's relationship with us; and then us pasting this onto our relationships with ourselves, others, and the world—all the while thinking that in doing so we are being "biblical." Consequently our understanding of God and the nature of our relationship with God has been distorted because, for so long, we have viewed this through a lens that is alien to Jesus Christ and as a result generated ideas and practices that are alien to the true heart of God. And this has been disastrous for both Christians and non-Christians alike.

However, I think we know what happens in *human relationships* when for example: parents paste perfectionist expectations onto their children; spouses expect their partners to be perfect husbands or wives, and mothers or fathers; teenagers believe they must have a perfect body appearance to be valued by others; ministers think they (and their families) have to be perfect Christian role models; and employees feel that unless they do a perfect job their colleagues and bosses will consider them second rate. These examples illustrate why this Platonic ideal of "perfection" has been so actively encouraged by people in power—including Church leaders. The idea that God's standard is perfection is such a potent motivator of effort and toil in others. Moreover, this is why it sits at the heart of so much modern marketing. The key thing in marketing is to sow seeds of doubt in people by highlighting some imperfection in their lives; and then promoting a product that promises to eliminate the offending imperfection—always of course for a price!

But perfection is an elusive goal—it always remains tantalizingly just out of reach. As the *Hope Project* truthfully tells us, "Even if we try we cannot be perfect." What this means—and this is the master plan of all successful marketing, and also, sadly, a lot of Christian expectation—is that this elusive goal of perfection keeps people in a perpetual state of unhappy hopefulness which ensures they keep on spending money and expending effort keeping the faith. And as I say, this has been devastating for Christians and non-Christian alike—although very good for the economy and religious institutions (until people eventually wise up to the game that is being played on them)!

It is so important we understand that this kind of perfection is an *abstract static state of being*. Abstract means it is an other-worldly ideal, rather than a this-worldly reality. Static means it allows for no movement, or change, or growth—and certainly for no mistakes, and learning from those mistakes. And state of being means it is a fully formed outcome, rather than something we journey toward over time. What this means is that this kind of perfection doesn't open up space for authentic relational encounters that involve real human beings here on earth to take place.

And so we really have to ask—if the expectation of this Christianized Platonic ideal of perfection is so disastrous for relationships between *humans*; why have so many Christians for so long been so willing to believe that *God* should require it in his relationship with us?

In chapter 1, I said:

> God *is* love and so God's love has no reason beyond itself. Therefore God does not use his love as a *technique* in order to achieve some other purpose that *isn't* love. As a result God never manipulates or coerces us into any way of being we do not freely choose. This is why God gives us time and space to develop and grow so that we may respond to him in freedom and integrity. Therefore God, in creating both us and the world, intends and enables a

history of encounter to take place that allows time and space for all the different dimensions of relationship to be experienced. God's love therefore creates room for us to experience development and growth, joy and sorrow, alienation and reconciliation, sin and grace, judgment and salvation.

But the trouble with this *Christianized* Platonic concept of perfection is that it doesn't allow any of these normal relational things to take place.

So let's rip these Christianized Platonic glasses off! When we do we notice that Genesis 1 doesn't use the word "perfection," but seven times tells us that the world and all it contains is "good." We notice that Genesis 2 doesn't use the word "perfection" either—but highlights something that isn't good—something that is causing *suffering* that therefore needs to *change*:

It is not good for the man to be alone. (Gens 2:18)

When we ditch Platonic *perfection* and return to biblical *goodness*—a very different picture emerges. Instead of understanding God's relationship with us as a perfect abstract static state of being—this sets us free to understand it as a good *concrete dynamic process of becoming*. Concrete means it is a this-worldly flesh and blood reality. Dynamic means it allows for movement, change, and growth—and also for mistakes, and learning. And process of becoming means it is something we mature in and journey toward over time. Most importantly, when we rip these distorting glasses off, this enables us to see with much greater clarity that for our theology to be genuinely *Christian* (and therefore not simply a *Christianized* version of something else) then it really is Jesus Christ—and Jesus alone—who must always be the starting point, heart and center, and end goal of all our thinking and acting in the world.

When we look to Jesus as he is revealed in the Bible—and as we experience his presence in our lives through the Holy Spirit—can we honestly say that typical Christian perfectionist evangelistic tracts faithfully describe him? Or to ask this another way, if the "perfect" god these tracts speak of became a human being and dwelt among us, who would this god incarnate resemble? Think of the woman caught in adultery in John 8—who, because of their "holy nature," insisted she "must be punished?" It was the Pharisees, not Jesus. Think of the story of the prodigal son in Luke 15—who "couldn't tolerate the sin" he had committed? It was the older brother, not the father.

Let me ask this another way; who used love as a technique to achieve some other purpose that wasn't love, and who sought to manipulate and coerce someone into a way of being that they did not freely choose? It wasn't Jesus in relation to the woman or the father in relation to his sons. Who gave time and made space to allow people to develop and grow so that they were able to respond in freedom and integrity; and who enabled a history of encounter to take place that allowed for all the different dimensions of loving relationship to be experienced? It wasn't the Pharisees in relation to the woman or the older brother in relation to his father and brother.

When we rip our Platonic "perfectionist" glasses off and understand that

> no one has ever seen God, but the one and only Son, who is himself God and is in closest relationship with the Father, has made him known. (John 1:18)

And simply ask, in what way does *Jesus* reveal true holiness, righteousness, and sinlessness of life it is abundantly obvious that in Jesus we see nothing of any kind of abstract philosophical or religious other-worldly "perfection." But we see plenty of this in the Pharisees. Think of the one who went to the temple to pray in Luke 18 reciting his great list of virtues and who "because of his holy nature couldn't tolerate the sin" of the tax collector. The true holiness of Jesus is found in a very this-worldly *goodness* of relational wholeness—not in an other-worldly abstract Platonic perfection.

Nevertheless we must acknowledge that the Bible *does* speak of the perfection of God and of our need for perfection also. In the Sermon on the Mount Jesus says:

> Be perfect, therefore, as your heavenly Father is perfect. (Matt 5:48)

However, if we insist on pasting a transcendent Platonic ideal of perfection onto this then this verse will crush us as it has crushed countless Christians before us. But the context makes it very clear what Jesus means. He is talking about God's relational faithfulness to *all* people—whether good or bad—and that, just as God's love is *inclusive* of all people, this is what God calls us to also.

One of the consequences of the widespread Christian practice of reading the Bible through a Platonic perfectionist lens is that the early chapters of Genesis have been made to carry a colossal theological weight that is alien to their intended purpose and, as a result, made to produce such bad fruit. This is certainly true, as we have seen, with the "perfectionist" emphasis given to the creation story from chapters 1 and 2. However, it is the story of Adam and Eve eating the forbidden fruit in chapter 3 that has been made to carry the greatest theological weight of all. Theologian Brian McLaren has called what has flowed out of this the "six-line model."[4] Although Christians are largely unfamiliar with this expression, it represents perhaps the weightiest theological idea in all of Christian history.

To appreciate the point I want to make it is helpful to first understand the difference between a *model* and a *paradigm*. Back in the day when I taught economics I would get my students to work with various models—the circular flow input/output model, the supply and demand model, the Keynesian macroeconomic multiplier model—all these being mathematical and graphical depictions explaining how the economic system is thought to work. There are two key things we must continually keep in mind about models. First—*models are not the real world*. Rather, they are theoretical depictions of the real world that we hope will help us better understand and, as a result, influence the real world in positive ways. Second—*models are always provisional*. This means we need to continually monitor how well the models we are relying upon stand up against data about how the real world is actually functioning.

If the gap between what the model is depicting and data from the real world becomes uncomfortably large, then we need to think about *modifying* the model—or perhaps even *ditching* it and replacing it with a better one. This gap has given rise to all manner of economist jokes. For example, an economist is someone who observes an event in the real world and then (with a worried frown) says, "That's all very well in *practice*, but how will it work in *theory*?" And the anxious mother who takes her son to a psychiatrist who gives his diagnosis, "Your son has absolutely no grasp of reality—there is no cure—he'll have to become an economist!"

But the trouble with *models*—especially useful ones—is that they risk becoming *paradigms*. A paradigm is a model that, in people's minds, is no longer a theoretical depiction of the real world—but the indisputable truth of how the real world actually is. What this means is that the model has turned into a totalizing intellectual framework—and in the case of the six-line model, a totalizing *theological* framework—that silences all other voices. As paradigms become embedded in wider culture they become like the air we breathe—something we are no longer consciously aware of and therefore something we no longer think to critically question—but instead

---

4. McLaren, *A New Kind of Christianity*, 33–45.

something we unconsciously accept as "just the way the world is." And this is what has happened with the six-line model.

It is therefore so important that we make ourselves consciously aware of it again *as a model*—which is what it actually is and therefore should be treated as being—so that we can critically question it and test how well it stands up against real-world data. Because the six-line model is a *theological* model this means that the real world data we must test it against is *Jesus Christ* as we understand Jesus from the Bible and in light of our experience of Jesus through the Holy Spirit.

So what is the six-line model? It is six lines on three levels.

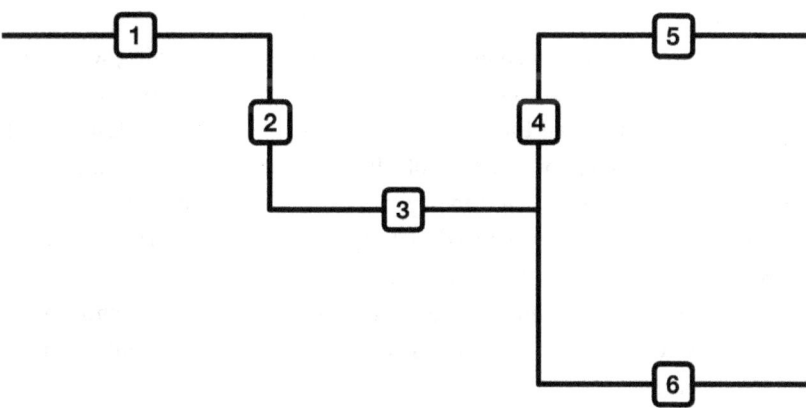

Reading the model horizontally from left to right depicts *time* and *eternity*. Line 1 represents all eternity past and lines 5 and 6 all eternity future. Line 3 represents normal historical time here on earth. Reading the model vertically from top to bottom depicts the three levels of *cosmological space*. Lines 1 and 5 are on level one which is *heaven*—the dwelling place of God; line 3 is on level two which is *earth*—the dwelling place of humans; and line 6 is on level three which is *hell*—the dwelling place of the damned and irredeemable. Lines 2 and 4 are the two decisive moments in the history of the cosmos that shape *all space* for *all eternity*. Line 2 is Genesis chapter 3 and line 4 is the end of age judgment.

And so—reading the model as a whole.

Line 1 represents God's perfect eternity in heaven on level one—that is, "perfect" in the *never changing* and *never suffering* Platonic sense we have been discussing. Coming in from the left, line 1 is infinitely long indicating that God's realm of heavenly perfection has extended unchanged from all eternity past. The last bit of line 1 as it comes into the picture just before it hits line 2 includes Genesis chapters 1 and 2—the creation of God's perfect level one dwelling in God's new world in the garden of Eden.

Line 2 represents Adam and Eve eating the forbidden fruit in Genesis 3. For Christians who accept the six-line model this event is regarded as a catastrophic cosmic disaster that has forever set God's creation on a collision course with hell on line 6. To underscore the gravity of this event it has often been described using ominous theological terms such as "Original Sin," "The Fall," and "Total Depravity." All of these expressions spelled with upper case letters—none of them, it should be noted, found anywhere in the Bible!

Line 3 represents normal history here on earth beginning with Genesis 4. It therefore includes the whole of biblical history. It also includes all other human history all the way up to the second coming of Jesus which terminates normal history. The twenty-first century is therefore somewhere on line 3—although no one can say precisely where. Throughout history Christians have generally believed that their particular century has sat close to where line 3 is terminated by line 4.

Line 4 depicts the end of age judgment that determines who spends all eternity future in the blessedness of heaven and who spends it in the torments of hell.

Line 5 represents the destination of the righteous who are taken to the heavenly perfection of level one where they enjoy an eternal existence of conscious blessedness with God. Line 5 therefore extends infinitely rightward for eon upon never changing and never suffering eon.

And line 6 is the destination of the impenitent wicked who are judged unworthy of heaven or earth and so are cast down into the depths of level three in hell. In the strong version of this model line 6 also extends infinitely rightward for eon upon never changing, but now always suffering, eon. However, in modified versions of the model, line 6 terminates at some point—either with the annihilation of the wicked or else with their ultimate redemption.

And so there it is—the six-line model—a theological model that for so many and for so long has been accepted as a totalizing paradigm that has deeply *shaped*—and in many ways deeply *traumatized*—the theological imagination of an entire culture; indeed, an entire civilization.

In order to better appreciate how the six-line model has shaped Christian thinking it is helpful to briefly survey how it has been understood throughout its near 1,900-year history. In the early period from around the mid-second century, when it first began to be formulated, it really was a model. In other words, it was openly discussed and debated as a way of understanding the biblical data concerning God's plans and purposes for the cosmos. Although, generally in the minority, there were nevertheless many Christians who believed the model didn't fit the data very well—that is, that it didn't cohere with Jesus Christ as we understand him from the Bible and as we experience him through the Holy Spirit. And so these Christians believed the model should be modified or ditched.

Nevertheless—and it is so important we appreciate this—although there was disagreement between different schools of Christian thought with respect to the six-line model, for the most part, it was respectful disagreement—and the debate this disagreement generated was conducted in the context of Christian unity. Therefore people didn't regard those they disagreed with as *heretics*. Rather, they accepted that Christians of goodwill could have different views on this profoundly important question. However, with the passage of time attitudes hardened—which, sadly, is so often the way. A decisive turn came in the fifth century with Augustine. Without question Augustine is the most brilliant thinker the church has produced and his influence on Western Christian culture is immense. Augustine was an ardent advocate of the six-line model in its strong form. He dismissively referred to those who believed that God's ultimate purpose is to reconcile all humanity and all creation to himself in and through Jesus Christ as—"the merciful-hearted."[5]

With Augustine the six-line model became a seldom-questioned paradigm that sunk deeply into Western Christian consciousness and, as a result, was simply accepted as the way the world actually is. During the medieval period and into the Reformation in the sixteenth century, Christian consciousness was the consciousness of all Western Europe and so the hope of heaven and the dread of hell dominated every aspect of public and private life. However, by the eighteenth century—with the revolution in thinking known as the Enlightenment—open atheism had become a social and political possibility and many took the opportunity to reject the whole business as being morally repugnant—God and all! This began the process of the secularization of society that we are so familiar with today. This dealt

---

5. Hart, *That All Shall Be Saved*, 1.

the six-line model a major blow from the point of view of its influence on wider secular culture.

The key event that dealt the model its second major blow—this time from the point of view of its influence on Christian faith—was World War I. The reports and photographs of hundreds of thousands upon hundreds of thousands of young men being slaughtered in the killing fields of Europe produced such a profound sense of abhorrence at such suffering and torment—*in this life at the hands of men*—that large numbers of Christian ministers could simply no longer, in good conscience, preach the traditional doctrine of hell as even more suffering and torment—*in the life to come at the hands of God*.

And so we come to the present. Preachers who remain active advocates of the six-line model tend to be those who, for the most part, are connected to or have been influenced by the Pentecostal revival that began at the beginning of the twentieth century. However, most mainstream churches have quietly dropped reference to the six-line model and so you seldom hear full-blooded fire-and-brimstone sermons on hell from them anymore. However, there are a growing number of theologians and preachers who, like me, believe that we need to be open and honest about this whole business and not just quietly drop reference to such a profoundly weighty and influential theological idea that still sits just below the surface of so much Christian thinking and behaving.

7

God's Good Creation
—so did anything go right?

IF WE ARE WILLING to set our Platonic "perfectionist" glasses aside and do our very best to read the story of the Bible—and especially Genesis 3— without this distorting lens, I believe there are two things in Genesis 3 that give us important clues concerning how the original ancient Hebrew readers would have understood this story. This paints a very different picture compared to the one painted by those who have adopted a "perfectionist" Christianized Platonic six-line model.

The first clue is that Genesis 3 begins with a snake that talks and the second is that the key human actors are naked, but don't know it. If this was any other book I think we would readily accept that these are clear literary signals that what we are reading is *not* actual history in a modern sense, but some kind of fairy tale, myth, or fable. But of course the Bible isn't "any other book" and Genesis 3 isn't "any other chapter." For Christians the Bible is the word of God and Genesis 3 is the one chapter that, more than any other, has been made to carry the colossal theological weight of the catastrophic cosmic disaster that has forever set God's creation on its collision course with hell. How we decide to read this chapter has monumental implications for how we understand God, how we understand the Bible as a whole, and how we understand God's relationship with his world—and in particular—the language and underlying theological presuppositions we employ to speak of these things.

Now I don't want to use the terms *fairy tale*, *myth*, or *fable* in relation to Genesis 3 because that is simply to impose our modern categories of thought upon this ancient text. But equally, we need to acknowledge that treating it as actual history in a modern sense is also to impose our categories of thought upon it. So what to do?

I believe we really do need to take seriously the fact that the story begins with a talking animal and involves naked humans who don't know they are naked. What I take from this is that we should therefore be open to reading it in a somewhat more imaginative and symbolic way than we would a strictly "historical" document. I believe we should be willing to consider reading it in a similar way to the way we read the parables of Jesus. Matthew tells us in 13:34–35:

> Jesus spoke all these things to the crowd in parables; he did not say anything to them without using a parable. So was fulfilled what was spoken through the prophet: "I will open my mouth in parables, I will utter things hidden since the creation of the world."

Which is rather interesting given that Genesis 3 is very much about Adam and Eve coming to the knowledge of things "hidden since the creation of the world"—in particular, the knowledge of good and evil.

What is important we understand is that a parable isn't "actual history"—or even "true" in the sense that, for example, there really was a son who demanded that his father give him his inheritance, went off to a faraway country where he blew it all in drunken debauchery, ended up in a pigpen and then, out of deeply painful process of soul-searching, began the long journey back to his true home. But something doesn't have to be true in a literal or historically accurate sense in order to be true in a theological or morally applicable sense. There are some truths that are far better conveyed in story form—or even as "myth"—rather than in a strictly factual way. This is because many truths are far better *discovered* than *told*. Many truths are actually wasted on us because we are not yet ready to receive them.

I think this is why Jesus used parables as his preferred method of teaching. A parable is a literary form that conceals—yet also reveals. It is therefore ideally suited to conveying truth about transcendent realities to a wide range of people of differing perspectives and maturities in a way that allows them to discover things about God, and about themselves, as and when and to the extent they are ready to receive them.

We should ask ourselves therefore—is there a parable Jesus tells that resembles Adam and Eve's disobedience against God in the garden. Is there a parable about someone taking something from their father they had no right to take, leaving home in disgrace, finding themselves in a harsh new reality far from home, and after much suffering taking a long journey back home—yet in all these things still subject to the fatherly care of God? Putting it like this the answer is of course "yes." The parable of the prodigal son in Luke 15 has many parallels with Genesis 3. It's a story of an ignorant and naïve young man who seizes possession of something he wasn't yet ready to receive—the story of an immature self-absorbed young man who has a great deal to learn about good and evil. But it is also the story of a loved child whose father allowed him to have what he desired even though he knew it would bring them both great suffering—and a very long and painful, but ultimately life-giving, journey back to his true home.

In this way both Genesis 3 and Luke 15 are telling the universal human story of ego and aspiration, sin and alienation, judgment and sorrow—all as part the long journey to grace and reconciliation, maturity and self-awareness, salvation and joy as we journey back to our true home in God. The story of Adam and Eve and the parable of the prodigal son are therefore stories that are woven deeply into the fabric of our human consciousness. And because God is the God who loves us—these stories are woven into the tapestry of the one overarching story of God's faithfulness to his creation. They are, therefore, two stories that, in their different ways, as Tim Keller so evocatively puts it, "whisper the name of Jesus." In this way they are stories of human aspiration and shame that are gathered up, reconciled, redeemed, and transcended in Jesus Christ.

What I believe we see in Genesis 3 therefore is not a catastrophic cosmic disaster that has forever set God's creation on a collision course with hell. But rather God—as any good, loving, and wise parent would—*warning* his children that the decisions they make in the world God has created have real consequences they will have to live with—consequences going forward that will significantly impact upon the nature of the relationship they have with God, with themselves, with each other in human community together with others, and with the world God has created. It is important we understand that in Genesis 1 God has already described his world as being "very good" and so the tree of the knowledge of good and evil and the snake are part of God's good creation and therefore not evil. Throughout Scripture we are repeatedly urged and warned to pursue goodness and shun evil, and therefore it is a vitally important part of our maturity that we to come to an understanding of good and evil. What this means therefore is not that God didn't want Adam and Eve to come to this knowledge—but that there is a right and wrong way of going about this vitally important process.

Every loving, good, and wise parent knows that there is a time and stage for imparting to their children knowledge about the harsh realities of the adult world, and that too much too soon and in the wrong way can be deeply traumatizing. It is certainly true that in Genesis 2:16–17

> The Lord God commanded the man, saying, "You may freely eat of every tree of the garden; but of the tree of the knowledge of good and evil you shall not eat, for in the day that you eat of it you shall die." (NRSV)

But what we see in chapter 3 is that, as the snake says, they *don't* die the day they eat of it. Indeed Genesis 5 tells us Adam lived until he was 930 years old. What actually happens the day that they eat of the fruit is that God reaches out to Adam and Eve in love asking them, "Where are you," carefully explains to them the consequences of what they have done, and then provides clothing for them as they enter the new reality they now confront.

Clearly their wanting to "be like God knowing good and evil" was—as it was with the prodigal son demanding his inheritance—an appalling act of arrogant presumption. It was a disobedient refusal to acknowledge God as lord. In casting them out of the garden—as it was with the prodigal son leaving home—a decisive turn takes place in the relationship and, as a consequence, much suffering lies ahead for both God and his human creatures. But what is so important we understand is that in consigning them to this long history of separation from their true place of belonging—*God does not stop loving them*! In their decision to reject God's lordship, God does not stop providing for them. In their desire to be their own lords and masters, God does not cease caring for them. In their decision to seize for themselves the judicial authority of God and become their own judges and saviors, God does not stop being gracious toward them, and in all this works toward a redemptive outcome for them.

Does this mean God wasn't telling the truth when he said, "For in the day that you eat of it you shall die"? But the ancient Israelites knew what kind of god God is—and they were very certain that he wasn't a Platonic god of "perfection" who never changed his mind about anything. But rather, as the prophet Jonah so beautifully expresses it in 4:2 (although *not* with praiseworthy *intent*):

> I knew that you are a gracious and compassionate God, slow to anger and abounding in love, a God who relents from sending calamity.

So God wasn't lying, but had changed his mind and relented from sending calamity and therefore did not punish Adam and Eve with immediate death because he is a gracious and compassionate God who is slow to anger and abounding in love.

Now I don't know how you feel about this. Perhaps like Jonah and the Pharisees, and the prodigal's older brother—and the writers of the evangelistic tracts we looked at earlier—you would prefer God *wasn't* this kind of god; and instead, as the tracts say, is a god who, "because of his holy nature must punish" people when they disobey him. And of course, if this really is the kind of god God really is then it would certainly make it easier to accept the traditional six-line model interpretation of Genesis 3. But for better or for worse—and I believe it is very much for better—the kind of god we are dealing with (or rather, the God who is dealing with us) is, as Jonah so rightly says:

> A gracious and compassionate God, slow to anger and abounding in love, a God who relents from sending calamity.

It is my conviction therefore that if we read the story of Adam and Eve through *this* lens—the lens of God's mercy and patience and kindness; rather than through the traditional lens of "Original Sin," "The Fall," and "Total Depravity"—then I believe a very different picture emerges. It is a picture that certainly doesn't *underestimate* the power and consequence of this thing the Bible calls "sin"—something a genuinely Christian theology must never do. But nor is it a picture that *overestimates* it either—something a genuinely Christian theology must also never do.

The second thing about Genesis 3 is that the key actors—Adam and Eve—are naked, but don't know they are naked, which very much suggests they are in a state of childlike innocence. Young children, up until a certain age, are utterly indifferent to clothing. Sometimes they happily wear clothes and sometimes they don't. Either way they are utterly without pride or shame and utterly without guile or pretence—their childlike innocence beautiful to behold. But of course a time soon comes when some developmental switch is turned on in their psyche such that, like adults, they become aware of their nakedness. As a result they feel the self-conscious embarrassment that instinctively prompts them to cover themselves. This is why nakedness has long been understood as a symbol of childlike innocence. So much the art that has come out of Christian Europe show angelic beings in the presence of God—*without clothes on*. In the theological imagination of these classic Christian artists—an imagination that has been shaped by Genesis 3—they understand that nakedness is symbolic of childlike innocence and wearing clothing acknowledgment of the shame that accompanies sin.

I believe this is what Genesis 3 is signalling—that Adam and Eve (prior to eating the forbidden fruit) are in a state of childlike innocence. As a consequence they are in the inevitable childlike naivety that always accompanies childlike innocence. They are both depicted as being utterly without pride or shame, utterly without guile or pretence, and utterly ignorant and naive. In her conversation with the snake Eve is totally trusting, completely unsuspecting, fully open and transparent, and entirely unguarded and gullible in her childlike naivety.

> "You will not certainly die," the serpent said to the woman. "For God knows that when you eat from it your eyes will be opened, and you will be like God, knowing good and evil." When the woman saw that the fruit of the tree was good for food and pleasing to the eye, and also desirable for gaining wisdom, she took some and ate it. She also gave some to her husband, who was with her, and he ate it. Then the eyes of both of them were opened, and they realized they were naked; so they sewed fig leaves together and made coverings for themselves. (Gen 3:4–7)

What innocent, naïve, gullible child could resist such an enticing temptation? It appeals at every level—the *physical* (it was good to eat); the *aesthetic* (it was pleasing to the eye); the *intellectual* (it was desirable for gaining wisdom); and the *spiritual* (her eyes would be opened and she would be like God). What child doesn't want to be like their parent?

If instead of reading this as actual history we understand it as a kind of parable telling a universal human story what is being depicted here is Adam and Eve transitioning from the unselfconscious innocence of childhood to the deeply problematic and conflicted world of adulthood. If we read this story symbolically instead of literally—as they are cast out of Eden this primal human couple are leaving the magical garden of their childhood and entering the cruel and harsh world of adulthood; and all the knowledge and awareness (both good and evil) that comes with adulthood.[1]

---

1. Jewish Study Bible, 17.

So much world story, literature, and song is about this hazardous transition from childlike innocence to adult knowledge and the great human longing to find our way back to this primal place of safety and belonging. But the way is closed!

> And the LORD God said, "The man has now become like one of us, knowing good and evil. He must not be allowed to reach out his hand and take also from the tree of life and eat, and live forever." So the LORD God banished him from the Garden of Eden to work the ground from which he had been taken. After he drove the man out, he placed on the east side of the Garden of Eden cherubim and a flaming sword flashing back and forth to guard the way to the tree of life. (Gen 3:22–24)

One way or another—whether we are consciously aware of it not, whether openly or secretly, knowingly or unknowingly; whether from out of our functionality or our dysfunctionality; whether witnessed by our brokenness or our wholeness—this is our universal human yearning: to find our way back to our true home with God. And this yearning has been hardwired into the very fabric of our beings and sits at the heart of all that we hope for, all that we do, and all that we strive toward.

Nevertheless, despite these clear literary signals in Genesis 3—the talking snake and the naked couple who don't know they are naked—most Christians have been predisposed by the six-line model to read this story through the lens of disobedience leading to cosmic catastrophe. It is therefore worth reflecting on the theme of obedience and disobedience *in light of Jesus Christ*. I conclude this chapter with six brief meditations on this theme.

First, as Paul reflects on Adam and Jesus, in Romans 5:19, he says:

> For just as through the disobedience of the one man [Adam] the many were made sinners, so also through the obedience of the one man [Jesus] the many will be made righteous.

And in 1 Corinthians 15:21–22:

> For since death came through a man, the resurrection of the dead comes also through a man. For as in Adam all die, so in Christ all will be made alive.

And so from the outset the New Testament wants us to understand that in whatever way Adam's disobedience harms us, the obedience of Jesus heals us.

Second, Hebrews 5:8 tells us:

> Son though he was, he learned obedience from what he suffered.

There are no shortcuts to this kind of obedience nor are there easy roads that take us there. It's a long and painful journey—one that requires our being stripped of our idealistic childlike religious certainties; learning what it means to take up our crosses daily and following Jesus; coming to the point of surrender where are willing to lose our lives for the sake of Jesus—and trusting that he will give them back to us again in a form that will best serve the higher obedience of love.

A while ago someone told me that, as a younger man, he had been engaged in full-time Christian ministry. He said that while keen, committed, and capable, he was also naïve concerning the harsh realities of the adult world and, as a result, was much too quick to judge. One day an older Christian took him aside and gently said, "Your problem is that you haven't suffered yet." And in the course of time he did suffer. And from out of the depths God graciously enabled him to still be keen, committed, and capable—but now much less naïve, much more compassionate and empathetic, and much, much slower to judge.

Third, the Pharisees provide us with the classic case study concerning what a life focused on religious law-obedience ends up looking like. The thing we must understand is that, for the Pharisees, their obedience to the law of God was not simply a matter of their own private spirituality. They were convinced that the entire nation lay under the wrath of God because, as a nation, the people were disobedient to the law of God. And so the Pharisees saw themselves, like Nehemiah, as God's righteous warriors whom God had called to get everyone to obey his law.

But here comes Jesus treating these outcasts and sinners like they brought down—not God's *judgment* and *wrath* on account of their disobedience—but God's mercy and love on account of God's covenant faithfulness. And this is what so enraged the Pharisees—Jesus seemed to go out of his way to undermine their national religious law-obedience project. He was just so slack around Sabbath observance; so loose about the food purity laws (so willing to welcome and eat with all the wrong kinds of people); and so prepared to violate the holiness code by touching lepers, dead people, women with issues of blood, and those possessed by demons.

My fourth meditation comes from Romans chapters 9 through 11. Paul's great question here is, "Why has Israel (for the most part) been disobedient to the gospel?" He goes on to reflect on Old Testament history and makes the scandalous point that there is nothing new in this—Israel has been disobedient from the outset! And then even more scandalously—Israel's disobedience has actually been God's *purpose* from the outset! But why would God do such a thing?

Paul sums up his argument in 11:32 saying:

> For God has bound everyone over to disobedience so that he may have mercy on them all.

The Pharisees were prisoners of the worst kind of disobedience—religious law-obedience. But what we learn from Genesis 3 is that the first people God made prisoners of disobedience so that he could show mercy to them both were Adam and Eve—the two primal humans who represent us all.

Now I don't want to encourage rebellion, but the truth is that too much obedience (and certainly the wrong kind of obedience) is actually a bad thing. The truth is that God isn't especially concerned that we be obedient—if he was, Jesus would have been a Pharisee! Rather, God's great concern is that we grow in Christlike maturity so that our capacity to receive and give love is enhanced and enlarged. In other words, God is concerned that, like Jesus, we learn the higher obedience of love through the things we suffer. Obedience is appropriate for the early stages of the journey toward maturity—that is, for children. But as we mature obedience becomes less and less relevant, and beyond a certain point, less and less helpful. This is because, when obedience has done its job of training in Christlike maturity as it is intended to, it withers away. And the great tragedy is that if obedience doesn't wither away when it should, then we risk becoming Pharisees in chains—as many sadly so often do.

Fifth, in Galatians 3:23–25 Paul says:

> Before the coming of this faith, we were held in custody under the law, locked up until the faith that was to come would be revealed. So the law was our guardian until Christ came that we might be justified by faith. Now that this faith has come, we are no longer under a guardian.

This is what every wise and loving parent understands—that there is certainly a time for children to be obedient if they are to progress on a healthy path toward maturity. However, that time comes to an end as they progress in maturity. The truth is that obedience is simply one of the training wheels of love—not the end goal of God's purposes for us. But as love matures, the time comes when we need to unbolt the training wheels—and that time is Jesus Christ. Moreover what every wise and loving parent also understands is that there comes a time when, in order to mature in a healthy way, every child actually *needs* to rebel against parental authority—the right kind of rebellion that is. And this is why every wise and loving parent gives their children something they *can* rebel against—without destroying themselves, which is sometimes what happens if their parents don't recognize this need.

I know a man who is a very talented musician. Many years ago as a young man his father called him back from overseas from the concert band he was playing in to manage the family farm. I remember him showing me his office. All around against the walls were his musical instruments, but they were unplayable—buried beneath boxes of farm accounts and paperwork. It was one of the saddest things I'd ever seen—a deeply symbolic tragic commentary on his life. If ever there was someone who needed to lovingly and firmly rebel against his father in order to progress toward healthy maturity it was this man.

And sixth, I invite us to consider the parable of the prodigal son (and his older brother) in Luke 15 as Jesus' commentary on obedience and disobedience. What the younger son did was clearly disgraceful and, as a result, both he and his father (and his family) suffered greatly because of what he did. But as Jesus tells the story, it wasn't the obedient older son who grew in maturity—rather it was the disobedient younger son. Through much suffering he grew in his ability to accept and receive his father's loving mercy. And I am convinced he would have grown in his ability to extend loving mercy to others as well. And here's the test—which of the two brothers would you go to if you needed to talk about your struggles, your feelings of unworthiness, the difficult relationship you have with your father, and your wondering if God could ever accept such a one as you? Give me the younger brother every time!

What this means, I believe, is that rather than seeing Genesis 3 exclusively as a story of disobedience that results in cosmic catastrophe I think it more faithful to the true heart of God, as this is revealed in Jesus, seeing it as a deeply insightful way in which ancient Israelites sought to understand their own humanity in light of the God they knew to be:

> A gracious and compassionate God, slow to anger and abounding in love, a God who relents from sending calamity. (Jonah 4:2)

Thinking about Genesis 3 as a parable allows us to imagine God saying to Adam and Eve—these primal humans who represent us all:

> I want you to come for a walk with me. It will seem to you like a very long walk. It is a long walk out of the garden of your childhood and into the wider world of adult reality. There is much I want you to learn, but here in the garden there is much that you are not yet ready or able to receive. But when you have learned the obedience of love from the things you must inevitably suffer, I will bring you back here to the garden—and the first thing I will give you is fruit from the tree of life.

8

Repentance
—so who needs to do it?

IN HIS DEEPLY INSIGHTFUL book *Falling Upward*, Richard Rohr comments:

> For Franciscans, Jesus did not need to change the mind of God about humanity, but he came to change the mind of humanity about God.[1]

Not only is this a deeply perceptive way of thinking about the *atonement*—that is, what God has done through Jesus Christ on the cross to reconcile us to right relationship or "at-one-ment" with God—it is also a very helpful way of thinking about the *message* God calls us to embody and proclaim.

Although the New Testament tells us repeatedly, "Jesus died for our sins," significantly, it never offers a precise account concerning the actual theological *mechanism* that accomplishes our salvation—it never explains precisely why God chose to save us from our sins in this particular way. This is something Charles Wesley had the humility and wisdom to recognize in his great hymn:

> 'Tis mystery all! The Immortal dies! Who can explore His strange design?

However, rather than providing a precise theological mechanism, what the New Testament gives us is all manner of *illustrations* and *metaphors* drawn from everyday life to help us picture what God has done for us

---

1. Rohr, *Falling Upward*, 172.

in the event of the cross. For example, Jesus is portrayed as: our *redeemer* who pays the ransom price to purchase our freedom from slavery; our *victor* who defeats our deadly enemy; our *sacrificial lamb* whose shed blood cleanses us from defilement; our *great physician* who heals our fatal disease by removing our body of death and transferring his life in all its abundance to us; our *good shepherd* who lays down his life to save us from wild animals and false shepherds; our *benefactor* who becomes poor in order to pay our great debt; a *seed* that dies in the ground thus producing a life-giving harvest; our *peacemaker* who overcomes our dysfunctional and alienated condition and reconciles us to right relationship with God; our *mother* who through great travail births us to new life—and so on.

But these metaphors and illustrations drawn from the slave market, the battlefield, the temple worship, medical practice, pastoral agriculture, loan contracts, horticulture, human relationships, childbirth, and so on—because they are drawn from our *human* experience they are therefore limited and imperfect. Nevertheless, God deems them sufficient such that, as we consider them *together*, our faith may have understanding. For the first thousand years Christians were largely content to accept the witness of the New Testament in relation to this. Consequently—although there were many ecumenical councils such as Nicaea in the fourth century and Chalcedon in the fifth that thrashed out carefully worded statements concerning the precise nature of the divinity and humanity of Jesus and the Trinitarian nature of God—there was never a council that tried to provide a particular theological account concerning *how precisely* God saves us from our sins.

However, in the eleventh century, Anselm of Canterbury sought to rectify this perceived deficiency. Anselm lived in Europe at the height of the medieval period and argued that God was really like a feudal lord whose honor has been offended by human sin and therefore requires *satisfaction* on account of this offense to his honor. This is because, as everyone knew, any self-respecting feudal lord whose honor has been offended has the right to demand satisfaction appropriate to his honor. What this means, Anselm argued, is that God simply cannot forgive out of nothing—it means that in order for God to pardon offense some form of satisfaction must be given sufficient to recompense the honor that is appropriate to God's status. In other words a price must be paid! Crucially, because God's honor is infinite the price that must be paid to satisfy this offended honor must also be infinite. This of course is the price that Jesus paid on the cross on our behalf—the infinite value of God's one and only son.

The upshot of Anselm's theory concerning the actual theological mechanism that accomplishes our salvation was to open this question up to all manner of theological speculation. Since the Reformation many Christians have taken one particular biblical metaphor and elevated it to the status of being the *primary*, or even *only* mechanism by which we are to understand the atonement and therefore the *primary*, or even *only* means by which we are to communicate the gospel. I refer to the penal substitution theory of the atonement—an idea drawn from the criminal justice system. In this portrayal God saves us by Jesus becoming our *criminal substitute* who takes our place before the bar of God's justice, bearing our guilt and punishment for crimes we have committed in order that we may not have to suffer the penalty that rightly belongs to us.

But the problem with elevating one particular metaphor (and therefore de-emphasizing the many others the New Testament uses) and turning this one metaphor into a precise theological *mechanism* (rather than simply accepting it as a serviceable *illustration* along with others) is that this way of viewing the atonement now has to do a great deal of work. As a consequence, the penal substitution theory of the atonement has frequently been pushed too hard and too far and, as a result, the central truth it seeks to convey has often been distorted. In particular it has led to a kind of "courthouse" Christianity that, when pushed too hard, has portrayed God as an obsessed legislator/judge whose law code has been violated and humans as lawbreakers in the dock of God's justice being prosecuted before this angry judge who is so bound to his own law-code that he can only ever respond to human sin within a *legal* framework of judgment, guilt, condemnation, and punishment. In this portrayal the law reigns supreme and all else must bow before it—even the mercy of God! Consequently, acquittal hinges upon—not the *grace of God* who is lord of all things (including his own law)—but finding *a legal mechanism* that enables the force of this supreme law to fall upon an innocent victim who is willing to take our place.

The penal substitution theory has sometimes been worked so hard that it has become profoundly unhealthy with disastrous consequences for how people have come to understand God and the way many Christians have sought to convey the message of the gospel to others. These portrayals typically lay great stress on human sinfulness, unworthiness, and guilt before a holy god who can only ever respond with wrath and punishment. However, because of the saving intercession of Jesus, this holy god is willing to transfer his wrath away from us and lay it instead upon Jesus, our substitute, who is punished on our behalf for every sin committed. We are then urged to come to this holy god of wrath as our Heavenly Father to seek his mercy and forgiveness. Moreover—and this is my key point—this way of understanding the cross pictures Jesus as the means by which God is *propitiated* or *appeased* and thereby the means by which God is conditioned into *changing his mind about us*.

Thinking about the cross in this way certainly allows us to speak of *Jesus* as our loving savior. However, my concern is about what it says of *God* as our Heavenly Father. In other words, what does this way of understanding the atonement say about the character of God and God's true disposition toward us? In the way this idea has often been presented, God's true disposition toward us too easily risks being portrayed as disappointment and therefore God as father risks looking like a disgusted and angry parent who can only be placated by punishing someone. The role of Jesus as the one who saves us from the wrath of this angry parent too easily risks looking like a devoted mother who is willing to "take a bashing" so that the children may be spared the punishment of a violent father. And our role in this too easily risks seeming like we have to carefully "tiptoe around God on egg-shells" in case we inadvertently provoke God's true underlying wrathful disposition breaking out against us all over again. Therefore, this portrayal of the cross—particularly if it is not balanced with the other ways the Bible uses to speak of it—too easily risks a construal of a violent and unpredictable god who is impossible to please, but who may nevertheless be rendered "loving" by self-sacrificial religious behavior—first on Jesus' part and then ours. Moreover, what this portrayal of the cross bears witness to is that, rather than saving us from *sin and evil*, what Jesus is actually saving us from is—*an angry God!* Most importantly there is nothing in this portrayal that speaks of *God's* love—nothing that reveals that God, in his very being, *is* love.

What should challenge our thinking with respect to this is that there is nothing in this portrayal that has anything in common with what Jesus tells us in the parables of the lost sheep and the prodigal son in Luke 15— two stories that are all about finding and joyfully restoring in love one who was lost, not counting the cost of this search and restoration, and—most significantly—*requiring no punishment for sin*. Two stories therefore that are not about God changing his mind about us, but our need to change our minds about God. And flowing out of this, about our need to change our minds about others also. As we have already seen from 2 Corinthians 5:16:

> So from now on we regard no one from a worldly point of view.

The New Testament reinforces this truth repeatedly. It never speaks of God reconciling himself to us—something that would require God changing his mind about us. Instead it speaks repeatedly of God reconciling us to himself and thus our need to be reconciled to God. Or more precisely, our need to recognize and accept that in Jesus Christ, God (like the shepherd in the story of the lost sheep and the father in the story of the prodigal) has *already* reconciled us to himself even while we were lost. But our problem (like the prodigal in the pigpen) is that we don't yet *know* or (like his older brother outside the banqueting hall) simply can't yet *accept* that God's reconciling grace toward us (and others also) can truly be this amazing!

Another way of saying "changing our mind" is to use the biblical word *repentance*. Repentance means a change of heart and mind that leads to a change in disposition and behavior. It means to consciously recognize and acknowledge the wrongness concerning how we have been living, resolving to change the direction we have been traveling, choosing to put our life under new management, and walking in a new direction with new values, goals, and measures of success. It really means *conversion*—and this is precisely what Jesus came in order to call us to. In entering upon his ministry following his baptism and temptation in the wilderness Jesus immediately began engaging with people, saying, "Repent and believe the gospel," and, "Follow me." He immediately began challenging people to rethink the direction of their lives in light of the gospel and urging them to put their lives under new management—that is, under the lordship of God. This is what Jesus came to do—not to change God's mind about us, but to change our minds about God—not to call *God* to repentance concerning his disposition and behavior toward us, but to call *us* to repentance concerning our disposition and behavior toward God.

But there is a deeper truth in this that is so important we take on board. In our own strength and by our own power, repentance is impossible for us to accomplish. In our own strength and by our own power, our natural instinct is to imagine that in order for God to accept us we must change ourselves. But our thinking this way immediately introduces two great falsehoods. First, that there is something we need to do to *condition* God into accepting us—that is, there is something we must do to make God change his mind about us. And second, that we are actually *capable* of changing ourselves such that we are rightly oriented toward and acceptable to God—that we have the ability to make ourselves right with God.

However, if we imagine that the onus is upon us to change ourselves sufficient to rightly orient ourselves to God, this weight of expectation risks either crushing us (if we think we fail) or else turning us into sanctimonious prats (if we think we succeed). But our thinking this way makes the whole burden of obligation fall upon *us*—that it is *our* repentance, *our* obedience, *our* holiness, *our* prayer, *our* worship, *our* faith, *our* hope, *our* love (or whatever human virtue we think most impresses God) that makes this whole mechanism work. Moreover, and most crucially, thinking this way completely bypasses Jesus Christ!

What is so important we understand is that the whole message of the gospel—and what it is that really does make it *good* news—is that God *already* loves us and therefore requires nothing from us in order to condition himself into being loving toward us. It is precisely *because* God already loves us that God has freely chosen in and as Jesus Christ to come to where we are, enter into our situation, stand in our place on our behalf, and from this place of solidarity to do for us what we are incapable of doing for ourselves. What this means is that, all that Jesus is and does, he is and does for us—in our name, and on our behalf. His coming from the Father; his baptism to fulfill all righteousness; his life of obedience to the Father; his faith, hope, and love; his integrity of being and moral courage; his doing justly, loving mercy, and walking humbly with God; his worship and prayer; and his death, burial, resurrection, and ascension—in all these things we are gathered up and included in Jesus Christ as our representative one before God. In an utterly amazing and mysterious *exchange* Jesus takes upon himself our sin and death and carries it away to the one place it can be destroyed forever and transfers to us his life and holiness as a gift of his grace. Jesus becomes all that we are in order that we may become all that he is. Our repentance therefore is not what we do to activate and actualize all this—rather our repentance is our response to becoming aware that this is what God has already done for us. When we learn by the revealing mercy of the Holy Spirit that Jesus Christ is both representing God's love to us and representing us to God in loving response—our repentance therefore is really us saying our human "yes" and "thank you" toward God in response to God's "yes" and "let it be so" toward us in Jesus Christ.[2]

What is so interesting in the story of the prodigal is that it ends with the older brother standing angrily outside the banquet hall and the question

---

2. For a beautiful description of this process, see Torrance, *Worship, Community & the Triune God of Grace*.

that is left hanging is—will he come to terms with his anger, let it go, and enter in and celebrate his father's kindness? Will this man (who represents us all) say his human "yes" and "thank you" toward his father in response to his father's "yes" and "let it be so" toward both him and his brother? But of course to do this requires that he change his mind toward his father (*and his brother*)—it requires a change of disposition and behavior on his part. It therefore requires that he repent of his previous certainties with respect to the angry judgments he has made concerning his father and his brother. It requires on his part a conscious and deliberate change in the direction he has been traveling, choosing to put his life under new management, and walking in a new direction with new values, goals, and measures of success. It really means that he must undergo a conversion! We see precisely the same thing in the story of Jonah also.

The key question that has been made to sit at the center of the penal substitution theory of the atonement concerns how an angry God can be persuaded to change his mind toward us—or as Martin Luther framed the question, how can we find a gracious God? I hope that we can now see that thinking this way is to get this whole business completely back to front. What we learn from Jesus (and which is so well illustrated in the story of Jonah and the story of the prodigal) is that the key question that sits at the center concerns, *not* how an angry *God* may be persuaded to change his mind toward us, but rather, how can an angry *human* be persuaded to change his mind toward God!

When we get angry something *always* breaks—indeed something *must* break! Something *physical* might break—perhaps furniture or someone's bones. A *relationship* might break—trust is broken and others now fear and avoid us. Our *health* might break—ongoing anger does terrible things to our physical and emotional well-being. Our *mental well-being* might break. In our anger so often we demonize others and dream up ridiculous scenarios in which they get what's coming to them and we of course are gloriously vindicated. But all this grossly distorts the truth and thus we risk descending into an abyss of utter unreality—a form of madness!

But not all anger is bad. Some of the things that get broken are things that *need* to get broken. Jesus often became angry at the hypocrisy and hardheartedness of people who used religion as a tool to manipulate others and glorify themselves. In his anger he broke the tables of the money changers who had turned God's temple into a hideout for robbers. In his anger he broke the bondage of disease and social alienation that kept people from participating in the abundant life God desires for all humanity. But it is so often the case that anger in *our* hands does not achieve a godly outcome and so, in our anger, we often end up breaking all the wrong things. However, God makes it very clear concerning the *one* thing he does want us to break. David tells us in Psalm 51:17:

> My sacrifice, O God, is a broken spirit; a broken and contrite heart
> you, God, will not despise.

God calls us to break our *pride.* God calls us to take ourselves in hand and repent. We are not helpless victims in the face of our own anger—we *can* and we *must* make life-affirming and not life-destroying choices. In our anger something is always *going* to break—but *what* will it be? Jonah the prophet was "angry enough to die" as he refused to rejoice in the mercy of God toward the people of Nineveh. The older son in the story of the prodigal was so angry he was willing to break his father's heart by refusing to celebrate the return of his brother. But in both stories a gentle voice of mercy pleads with an angry man and in both cases we don't know how it ends. We don't know what breaks. We don't know whether the path of repentance is chosen or rejected.

Is it the relationship between the prophet and his God that breaks? Does the prophet's health break and so he really does get his death wish? Or is it the prophet's *hard-heartedness* that breaks as he learns to rejoice in the mercy of God upon his enemies? Is it the relationship between the older son and his father that breaks? Does the older son break free of his imagined slavery to his father and alienate himself from his family as he finally gets his wish to feast with his friends? Or is it his *resentment* that breaks as he learns to celebrate the loving-kindness of his father by accepting and rejoicing in his younger brother's return? Do these stories end with a broken and contrite heart that God does not despise or do they end with an angry man's pride fully intact and unbroken as he stands triumphantly unbowed and unrepentant amid the ruins of his broken relationships?

These stories don't tell us how they end because they are open invitations to each of us to examine our own hard-heartedness, resentment, and anger, and how we want our own stories to end—whether we truly desire the atonement that God has accomplished for us in Jesus Christ and therefore what *precisely* we will choose to break. In our anger something *will* break, *must* break, and *needs to* break—but what will it be?

9

I Am the Man
—so what is God doing about it?

THE STORY OF JONAH and the parable of the father's two sons are making the same point. God delights to show kindness and mercy—especially to the very ones that religious people so often judge and condemn as being unworthy of God's grace. This is something Jonah *recognized* with perhaps more clarity than any other prophet—yet may never have actually *accepted*. We read in 4:1–3 that in response to God's mercy to the people of Nineveh:

> To Jonah this seemed very wrong, and he became angry. He prayed to the Lord, "Isn't this what I said, Lord, when I was still at home? That is what I tried to forestall by fleeing to Tarshish. I knew that you are a gracious and compassionate God, slow to anger and abounding in love, a God who relents from sending calamity. Now, Lord, take away my life, for it is better for me to die than to live."

What a profound insight into the true heart of God. Jonah knew and accepted at a deep theological and spiritual level the gracious compassion of God in relation to his own interests, but recoiled at the thought that God would abound in love and therefore relent from sending calamity upon those he despised. Part of the problem for religious people, like Jonah and the older brother, is that God's kindness and mercy seems so extravagantly generous, so undeserved—so *prodigal* (and in this way so *unfair*)—that it causes them to be so offended and scandalized they become angry. Perhaps,

I AM THE MAN—SO WHAT IS GOD DOING ABOUT IT?

like Jonah, even angry enough to die. This is why to Jonah God's mercy seemed very wrong.

At the heart of anger is judgment—our inner conviction that we have the right to judge others. This goes right back to the first human sin in the garden of Eden—our desire to be like God knowing good and evil and therefore our human desire to seize the judicial authority of God and become judges of others, of ourselves, and even of God. As we survey the wickedness of the world we take eager possession of the knowledge of good and evil and we are not reluctant to use it. This knowledge gives us great moral certainty and so we feel entitled to pass judgment on all manner of things. However, one of the consequences of possessing the knowledge of good and evil is that it so often causes us to become not simply judges—but *angry* judges.

Moreover, our angry judgment is always accompanied by a strong sense of self-justification and self-righteousness. We exert great effort to convince ourselves and others that we are in the right and they are in the wrong. But listen to what Paul says in Romans 2:1–4:

> You, therefore, have no excuse, you who pass judgment on someone else, for at whatever point you judge another, you are condemning yourself, because you who pass judgment do the same things. Now we know that God's judgment against those who do such things is based on truth. So when you, a mere human being, pass judgment on them and yet do the same things, do you think you will escape God's judgment? Or do you show contempt for the riches of his kindness, forbearance and patience, not realizing that God's kindness is intended to lead you to repentance?

God sent Jonah to preach to Nineveh. Nineveh was the capital of Assyria and the Assyrians were among the cruelest oppressors of the Israelites in Old Testament times. Jonah hated the Assyrians with a vengeance and this is why he wanted to have nothing to do with an evangelistic mission to Nineveh—he didn't want God to show them *mercy*. What Jonah wanted was for them to *rot in hell*! He relished the thought that they would suffer and perish. He angrily judged them for doing to Israel precisely what he wanted God to do to them. In essence he was no different to them—he judged them, yet in effect did the same himself.

In the same way the older brother was outraged that his younger brother should have seized his freedom, gone off, and had a good time with his friends far from home. He angrily judged him and then was angry with his father for showing him kindness. Yet, like Jonah, in his anger he reveals that this is exactly what he himself wanted to do—he also wanted to seize his freedom and go off and have a good time with his friends:

> Look! All these years I've been slaving for you and never disobeyed your orders. Yet you never gave me even a young goat so I could celebrate with my friends. (Luke 15:29)

In essence he also was no different to his brother—he judged him yet in effect did the same himself. In this way, in our angry judgment-making, what we actually do is reveal our own secret hearts—we actually say far more about ourselves than about others! In this way we confirm the truth of what Paul says:

> You, therefore, have no excuse, you who pass judgment on someone else, for at whatever point you judge another, you are condemning yourself, because you who pass judgment do the same things.

But Paul's purpose is not to expose us all as hypocrites and then leave us to stew in our own angry juices. God's purpose in all this is to call us to *repent* of our anger and to repent of the judgment-making that lies at the root of our anger. God's purpose therefore in exposing us all as moral hypocrites is to break our pride.

> My sacrifice, O God, is a broken spirit; a broken and contrite heart you, God, will not despise.

At the center of Paul's purposes in this part of Romans is 2:4:

> Or do you show contempt for the riches of his kindness, forbearance and patience, not realizing that God's kindness is intended to lead you to repentance?

Jonah showed contempt for the riches of God's kindness toward the people of Nineveh by refusing God's call to preach the mercy of God among them, wanting to enjoy the spectacle of their destruction he so fervently hoped for, and by having more concern for his own comfort than the lives of 120,000 people. The older brother showed contempt for the riches of his father's kindness toward his younger brother by being utterly unaware of the pain of his father's broken heart and his daily desire for his son's return, refusing to participate in his father's joy at his son's return and thus reproducing in himself a new chapter of alienation in the life of his family, and humiliating his father in front of his guests that in its own way was every bit as disgraceful as the original behavior of his younger brother.

However, Paul urges us all: don't show contempt for God's kindness by behaving in these ways; don't show contempt for God's kindness by perpetuating a moral life of angry judgment-making upon the very people God is merciful toward. "Don't you realize that God's kindness is intended to lead you toward repentance?" he asks. But what is so important we understand is that the extraordinary point Paul is making is that it is not simply God's kindness toward *us* that is intended to lead *us* to repentance—it is God's kindness toward *other people* that is intended to lead *us* to repentance also! Moreover it is especially God's kindness toward the sort of people that we religious people are so prone to angrily judge that is intended to lead *us Christians* to repentance!

How does God speak truth to powerful, unrepentant, and pride-filled religious people who are unlikely to welcome the truth God seeks to convey? How does a prophet of God speak truth concerning the bad faith of a powerful, angry judgment-making, unrepentant, and pride-filled king—*to that very same king*? In 2 Samuel 11 and 12 we read of Nathan the prophet doing precisely this. He does so by telling David a *story*. It is a story about bad faith—a story that conceals its true meaning—a story that David thinks is about the terrible behavior of someone else. Nathan tells him a tear-jerking story about a rich man's bad faith in killing a poor man's pet lamb.

Nathan told this particular story because he knew that David understood precisely how it felt to be violated by powerful others on account of his experience with King Saul—and also because he knew how deeply David cared about lambs. Nathan knew it was a story David would empathetically and compassionately identify with, not just at a head level, but at a deep heart level also. Moreover, this wasn't a private word in David's ear. Nathan tells this story in open court where he comes publicly seeking the king's verdict of righteousness concerning a great wrong that has (allegedly) been done in the land. Who else but the king is responsible for making such righteous judgments thus ensuring that the truth of God is not suppressed by human unrighteousness?

Predictably, the blatant wrongness of the rich man's behavior outraged David. The legal code of ancient Israel didn't allow the death penalty for stealing—but right now David fervently wished it did:

> David burned with anger against the man and said to Nathan, "As surely as the Lord lives, the man who did this must die! He must

> pay for that lamb four times over, because he did such a thing and had no pity." (2 Sam 12:5-6)

David is morally outraged. The rich man's utter lack of empathy toward his neighbor, his flagrant abuse of power, and his arrogant sense of entitlement so enrages David's sense of righteousness that he launches into a great public rant in which he totally condemns the man. His guilt being so self-evidently obvious David thinks nothing of judging and condemning him in his absence, contrary to the law that required all things to be confirmed by two or more witnesses.

Now in telling his story, in 2 Samuel 12:4 Nathan says:

> A traveller came to the rich man, but the rich man refrained from taking one of his own sheep . . .

This word "refrained" translates a Hebrew word which means "to have compassion for" and therefore "to save or spare" and is best translated as "to have mercy" or "pity" upon. Consequently, because the rich man felt great compassion toward his own livestock he wanted to save his own sheep from the stew pot and so he had mercy on his flock. He had pity upon them and spared them—and killed and cooked his neighbor's lamb instead!

This is precisely what so enraged David. What sort of man could feel this deep sense of compassion toward thousands of his own sheep yet not have the slightest compassion for someone else who had just one? Therefore David picks up and uses this exact same word when he pronounces his judgment on the man.

> The man who did this must die! . . . because he . . . had no pity—
> [because he had no compassion and therefore no merciful desire to spare the poor man's lamb].

Except what David actually means is that the man deserves to die precisely because he *did* have pity. He deserves to die precisely because he *does* know exactly what it is to experience and feel and know mercy—*when his own interests are at stake*—but then utterly abandons or forgets or suppresses the mercy he knows so well when it's someone else's interests that are at stake. It is for *this* reason that in David's judgment the rich man is utterly without excuse!

It wasn't as though the rich man was just some heartless, ignorant brute who didn't know any better—someone who cared nothing for sheep, his own or anyone else's (which is bad enough). But what made the rich man's behavior so much worse than mere stealing was precisely because he *wasn't* a heartless, ignorant brute and because he *did* know better. He knew better because he himself was a man who knew what it was to love and have compassion, but who then totally suppresses this knowledge when it comes to someone else.

It is exactly this that lies at the heart of the second greatest commandment. In Matthew 22:37–39 Jesus commands:

> "Love the Lord your God with all your heart and with all your soul and with all your mind." This is the first and greatest commandment. And the second is like it: "Love your neighbor as yourself."

This is precisely what the rich man failed to do. He certainly knew how to love himself; he had tender compassion and mercy in relation to his own interests. But his great failing was that he didn't transfer to his neighbor this same tender compassion and mercy he had toward himself.

But as we know it was just a *story*—there was no rich man who had abused his power in order to steal a poor man's lamb. There was no man who deserved to die because, despite knowing better through his own experience of having received mercy in his own life, he nevertheless had no mercy for someone else . . . *or was there?*

> The man who did this must die! . . . because he . . . had no pity [declares David in his moral certainty]. You are the man! [replies Nathan].

And with these four words Nathan closes the trap. Suddenly David realizes that Nathan's story isn't about someone else—it's about *him*!

This is the thing; when we think a story is about someone else's bad behavior—like David, like Jonah the prophet, and like the prodigal's older brother—our moral indignation and angry judgment-making goes into over-drive. We see the truth of their situation with complete moral clarity and our righteous judgment is swift, certain, and fearless. But when we discover that the story is actually about us—about *me*; that *I* am the man—suddenly everything changes!

The fundamental religious law of the universe is that the righteous will live and the wicked will die—that the one who deserves God's favor is the person who is innocent of evil, and the one who deserves to be condemned by God is the person who practices idolatry and injustice. The reason we know this law is true is because it is confirmed by the force of the biblical witness with all its laws and commands in all their frightful purity and terrifying holiness. We also know this law to be true because there is an instinctive knowledge within us—the moral compass within us, our conscience—that convinces us that in order to be pleasing to God we must obey his commands. Moreover we know this law to be true because it is the judicial and psychological basis upon which our inner persecutor launches his every accusation against us—a judicial and psychological presupposition we seldom pause to question. But not only do we *know* the fundamental religious law of the universe to be true—and this is the truly crazy thing—we actually *want* it to be true. This is especially so when we experience evil behavior from others that we are on the receiving end of! When this happens we cry out against the injustice of others for the justice of God—for God to condemn and punish those who are violating us and to vindicate us who are (of course) innocent and good and righteous.

The religious psychology of David makes for fascinating study, particularly how this was shaped by his experience of being persecuted by King Saul. Many of David's psalms reflect this experience. Take Psalm 59, for example. The title gives the context: "When Saul had sent men to watch David's house in order to kill him." David cries out for the justice of God against the wickedness of Saul in vv. 1–5, saying:

> Deliver me from my enemies, O God; be my fortress against those who are attacking me. Deliver me from evildoers and save me from those who are after my blood. See how they lie in wait for me! Fierce men conspire against me for no offense or sin of mine, Lord. I have done no wrong, yet they are ready to attack me. Arise to help me; look on my plight! You, Lord God Almighty, you who are the God of Israel, rouse yourself to punish all the nations; show no mercy to wicked traitors.

David's religious psychology comes straight out of the fundamental religious law of the universe—save me, O God, because I am righteous and punish them because they are evil! Notice the last part of v. 5:

> Rouse yourself [O God] . . . show no mercy to wicked traitors!

But the thing that becomes especially interesting in David's religious psychology is when he *himself* becomes a wicked traitor—when he has an adulterous affair with the wife of one of his army officers and then has him assassinated in order to cover it up. In other words when he discovers, in the words of Nathan the prophet, that "he is the man!" We read David's response to this deeply painful revelation in Psalm 51. Again the title gives the context, "A psalm of David. When the prophet Nathan came to him after David had committed adultery with Bathsheba." Notice how he begins (v. 1):

> Have mercy on me, O God.

Now wait a minute, David—when you were the *victim* of the murderous plans of King Saul your prayer was, "Rouse yourself [O God] . . . show no mercy to wicked traitors!" But now that you have been exposed as a wicked traitor yourself your prayer is, "Have mercy on me, O God." So which way do you want it to be, David? What sort of god do you want God to be—one who shows *no* mercy to wicked traitors or one who *does*?

What is so very interesting in David's religious psychology—and so relevant to us—is that when he saw himself as an innocent victim of the evil behavior of others, he was more than willing to invoke the fundamental religious law of the universe. In Psalm 59 he says:

> Deliver me from evildoers and save me from those who are after my blood. See how they lie in wait for me! Fierce men conspire against me for no offense or sin of mine, Lord. I have done no wrong, yet they are ready to attack me.

David's appeal to God is based on his own innocence—that because he is righteous he deserves to live and because these others are wicked they deserve to die. But notice how this religious law disappears from view when David now recognizes that he *also* is a wicked traitor—that "he [also] is the man." In Psalm 51:1 he says:

> Have mercy on me, O God, according to your unfailing love; according to your great compassion blot out my transgressions.

What is the basis of David's appeal now—now that he knows that he *also* is numbered among the wicked? David realizes that he can no longer appeal to his own righteousness and so, wisely and humbly, he appeals to *God's* righteousness. His appeal to God is no longer on the basis of *his own* innocence and virtue, but on the basis of *God's* unfailing love and great compassion—God's covenantal *chesed* faithfulness.

Now what is so important for us to understand is that, in praying his prayer, "Have mercy on me, O God, according to your unfailing love; according to your great compassion," what David is really praying is that God will suspend, overturn, and abolish (or else somehow *transcend*) the fundamental religious law of the universe—that God will utterly put an end to the law that it's only the righteous who will live and the wicked who will die. What is even more important for us to understand is that we should be profoundly grateful that God has answered David's prayer with an emphatic "yes" and "let it be so" in the gospel of Jesus Christ. This is the good news that, in and as Jesus Christ, it was righteous God himself who died in order that an unrighteous humanity might live. As we have already seen, Paul expresses this fundamental truth in 2 Corinthians 5:21:

> God made him who had no sin to be sin for us, so that in him we might become the righteousness of God.

This is the gospel which is God's power to save *all* who believe (and therefore not simply all who are innocent of evil) and which reveals *God's* righteousness (and therefore not our own).

In Romans 10:1–4 Paul directly addresses the ancient Jewish (which is really the natural human religious) version of the search for a sufficient righteousness by which they might live:

> Brothers and sisters, my heart's desire and prayer to God for [the Israelites] is that they may be saved. I can testify that they have a zeal for God, but it is not enlightened. For, being ignorant of the righteousness that comes from God, and seeking to establish their own, they have not submitted to God's righteousness. For Christ is the end of the law so that there may be righteousness for everyone who believes. (NRSV)

The religious history of the world could very well be written under this heading:

> Being ignorant of the righteousness that comes from God, and seeking to establish their own, they have not submitted to God's righteousness.

This is the story of all natural human religious endeavor—seeking to establish our own righteousness. This is the story of the human search for a gracious God—seeking some basis within ourselves whereby we can come to God with something we can appeal to, something we can hold up and take pride in that we hope God will respond with favor to. This is the sad story of human religious elitism—seeking something that will allow us to distinguish ourselves from those who we judge have no righteousness within themselves to appeal to and therefore something that will form the basis upon which we can appeal to God to treat "*us*" differently from "*them*."

However, what we should be very clear about is that if the thing that we cherish most dearly in all our religious endeavors—like Jonah and the older brother—is our desire to see wicked people excluded from the life of God; then what this means is that we have chosen to live by the fundamental religious law of the universe which carries the ominous implication, "Show no mercy to evil traitors," and what this might ultimately mean for us when it is finally revealed that "I (also) am the man"! But if instead the thing that we cherish most dearly is our desire to receive God's mercy (and to extend this to others because we know that we also are numbered among the wicked) then what this means is that we have chosen to live by the gospel of God's grace which has the life-affirming promise; "Christ is the end of the law so that there may be righteousness for everyone who believes." As the Apostle Paul sums his great theological argument up in Romans 11:32:

> For God has bound everyone over to disobedience so that he may have mercy on them all.

Or as we may now express this in light of David's realization:

> For God has revealed that we are all "the man" so that he may have mercy on us all.

10

The Righteousness of God
—so is this a good thing or a bad thing?

In Romans 10 the Apostle Paul speaks of his fellow Israelites as having "a zeal for God that is not enlightened" and "being ignorant of the righteousness that comes from God, and seeking to establish their own." He uses this language because, as he surveys the story of ancient Israel and their history of religious endeavor, it reflects so well the legalism, elitism, and judgmental condemnation (of both self and others) that inevitably goes with ignorance of the righteousness that comes from God and the consequential human enterprise of seeking a self-established righteousness. However, I suspect Paul uses this language because it also reflects so well his own ignorance, as Saul the Pharisee, concerning his own unenlightened zeal in relation to God's righteousness—and the great energy he invested in seeking to establish his own. As we have seen, he concludes his commentary on this doomed search for self-established righteousness by pointing to the enlightenment that comes from the gospel:

> Christ is the end of the law so that there may be righteousness for everyone who believes. (Rom 10:4)

This is how Paul the Apostle (who used to be Saul the Pharisee) came to understand the saving work of Jesus Christ—"righteousness for *everyone* who believes."

How much energy has been expended over the course of human history determining and policing religious boundary lines in order to demarcate

The Righteousness of God—So Is This a Good Thing or a Bad Thing?

those who are judged to be *inside* God's favor from those who are *outside*? David in Psalm 15:1 asks this religious boundary determining question:

> Lord, who may dwell in your sacred tent? Who may live on your holy mountain?

This is a question about who is inside and who is outside of God's favor and how we may distinguish one from the other. From the point of view of our natural human religious instincts, David's answer doesn't really surprise us. The answer he gives consists of a list of virtues that those who are inside are expected to practice and vices they are expected to avoid. In other words, David's answer consists in having a zeal for God that is enlightened—*not* by the knowledge of Jesus Christ—but by the fundamental religious law of the universe that is ignorant of the righteousness that comes from God and which therefore seeks to establish its own.

Psalm 15 reflects the religion of Israel about a thousand years before God's revelation of himself in and as Jesus Christ. In the religion of ancient Israel, faithful Jews believed that people were either righteous or wicked. The righteous were those who were obedient to God; those, as the psalm says, "whose walk is blameless" (which is a rather high standard to maintain). The wicked, on the other hand, were those who lived in violation of God's commands—those who, as the psalm suggests, slander others, do wrong to their neighbors, don't keep their promises, extort money through high interest rate loans, and who accept bribes to pervert justice against the innocent.

The outcome of these two ways of life was clear cut—the righteous would be welcomed into the presence of God and be considered worthy to dwell in God's sanctuary; the wicked would be outcasts, despised and rejected, and forever banished from God's holy hill. However, what this came to mean is that in the religion of ancient Israel not only did the righteous person reject wicked-*ness* as a way of life—they also rejected wicked *people* as human beings. They drew an absolute distinction between themselves, whom they (of course) considered righteous, and those others they considered wicked. This attitude is expressed in v. 4 of Psalm 15—the person considered a fit candidate to dwell in God's sanctuary was he who:

> Despises a vile man but honors those who fear the Lord.

What this reveals is that this whole business of determining and policing religious boundary lines inevitably ends up revolving around how *insiders* behave toward those who they judge to be *outsiders*. So often from their secure place of self-established righteous insider-ness they "despise" these people *as people*. What this means therefore is that even though Psalm 15 appeals to and confirms so much that sits comfortably with our natural human religious instincts—nevertheless, in light of Jesus Christ, God calls us to reject the fundamental religious law of the universe that undergirds it. Moreover, the reason we have to reject the theology that sits at the heart of Psalm 15 is because of the fact that as Paul tells us in Romans 10:4:

> Christ is the end of the law so that there may be righteousness for everyone who believes.

In other words, the reason we have to reject the theological assumption that sits at the heart of Psalm 15 is because in the gospel of Jesus Christ *God himself* has rejected it.

This attitude of despising people who are thought to be vile in God's eyes was all too prevalent at the time of Jesus. We see it especially in the Pharisees. A good example of this is in Luke 18 where Jesus tells a parable in order to confront this attitude. Here Jesus teaches us that entitlement to come into the presence of God and to offer worship—contrary to Psalm 15—is actually *not* a matter, like David, of being able to recite a long list of good religious things we do and bad things we don't. In other words, it is not a matter of us establishing our own righteousness, but instead submitting ourselves to God's righteousness. This parable, in my view, may be read as Jesus' commentary on Psalm 15—a parable that asks the same boundary-determining and policing question David asked concerning who is on the inside with God. Notice how Luke introduces this parable in 18:9:

> To some who were confident of their own righteousness and looked down on everyone else, Jesus told this parable.

Jesus told this parable to people who had very much taken the theology of Psalm 15 to heart. These people expended great religious energy practising its virtues and avoiding its vices so that they could be "confident of their own righteousness" and how they should behave toward those they consider outsiders by "looking down on" or "despising" them. But unlike the answer David gave, the answer Jesus gives totally surprises us—at least it *should* surprise us. It is totally and utterly radical, controversial, and scandalous because it completely violates our natural human religious instincts because it bypasses and renders redundant the fundamental religious law of the universe. The answer Jesus gives surprised the people of his day because it bypasses and renders obsolete the sacred idea that we have to establish our own righteousness.

In the first-century Jewish world, the Pharisees were religious professionals who fervently committed themselves to obeying the law of Moses and were hugely respected by ordinary believers—a bit like ministers, priests, and pastors are in certain religious corners of our world. But tax collectors were collaborators with the Roman Empire who sucked the economic and spiritual life of the nation—a bit like immigrants, gang members, and homosexuals are thought to do in certain religious corners of our world. The Pharisee in Jesus' parable was clearly well-schooled in Psalm 15 and therefore, in his prayer, recites before God an impressive list of his religious accomplishments—the virtues he practiced and the vices he avoided. He even expresses deep gratitude concerning how blessed he is—he thanks God that "I am not like this tax collector." Whereas all the tax collector could manage was to stand at a distance and not even look up to heaven, but beat on his breast and say, as David learned to say, "God, have pity on me, a sinner"—and in this way become a role-model for Christian prayer ever since.

However, our problem as twenty-first-century Christians is that Jesus' answer no longer surprises or offends us. We are no longer shocked and scandalized by how radically he revises and reinterprets the standard religious answer to this boundary-determining question. In 18:14 he says:

> I tell you that this man [the tax collector] rather than the other [the religious professional] went home justified before God.

What we must realize is that the crowds who heard Jesus say this would have been utterly astounded that it was the gang member and *not* the Christian minister who was justified, or righteous, or in right relationship with God! Some (like the Pharisees) would have been astounded and *utterly scandalized*, whereas others (like the tax collectors) would have been astounded and *utterly overjoyed*. Those who, as Paul expresses in Romans 10, were "ignorant of the righteousness that comes from God, and seeking to establish their own" would have been appalled at the thought that God could consider such a one as this tax collector an insider. But those who had come to understand that "Christ is the end of the law so that there may be righteousness for everyone who believes" would have been overjoyed.

This is precisely what Paul is doing in Romans 1:16–17 when he says:

> For I am not ashamed of the gospel, because it is the power of God that brings salvation to everyone who believes: first to the Jew, then to the Gentile. For in the gospel the righteousness of God is revealed—a righteousness that is by faith from first to last, just as it is written: "The righteous will live by faith."

Paul speaks of everyone who believes; first to the Jew—and then to the Gentile. We need to understand this as meaning: first to the Christian minister, priest, and pastor—and then to the tax collector, gang member, and immigrant; first to the person who has a zeal for God that is unenlightened—and then to all those that religious people so often look down upon and despise; first to those who need God's mercy the most because of their religious tendency to be confident of their own righteousness—and then to all those who suffer under the weight of religious bigotry and abuse. Understanding this in these terms is so important because the gospel puts people right with God in exactly the same way that Jesus said the tax collector was put right—not by our ability to recite an impressive list of religious accomplishments, but simply by acknowledging our *need for* and then *accepting* the righteousness that comes from God.

But note carefully the *sort* of people the gospel has the power to save. It is:

> Everyone who believes.

It is so important we understand and take to heart that when Paul says "everyone who believes" he really does mean *everyone*. The astounding utterly *scandalous* and utterly *joyful* extent of this "everyone" is Paul's major theme in Romans. This "everyone" must be understood in the same radical way in which Jesus reread and reinterpreted Psalm 15 to include the likes of tax collectors as being recipients of God's grace as well. We can follow the progress of Paul's "everyone" and "all" in Romans as follows:[1]

- (1:16) I am not ashamed of the gospel, because it is the power of God that brings salvation to *everyone* who believes: first to the Jew, then to the Gentile.
- (3:22–24) There is no difference between Jew and Gentile for *all* have sinned and fall short of the glory of God, and *all* are justified freely by his grace through the redemption that came by Christ Jesus.

---

1. Emphasis added.

The Righteousness of God—so is this a good thing or a bad thing?

- (5:18) Consequently, just as one trespass resulted in condemnation for *all people*, so also one righteous act resulted in justification and life for *all people*.
- (10:4) Christ is the end of the law so that there may be righteousness for *everyone* who believes.
- (11:32) For God has bound *everyone* over to disobedience so that he may have mercy on *them all*.

What this means is that when Paul says "all people" and "everyone" he is emphasizing the way the gospel breaks down and obliterates every human distinction by which we try to determine and police religious boundaries between those we consider insiders and outsiders—between those we think are included in the grace of God and those we think aren't. In Paul's day the all-too-obvious distinction was between Jews and Gentiles. Today we must understand that what he is saying applies to *any* and *every* distinction we make between people—distinctions based on race, culture, ancestral privilege, religious law-obedience, gender, sexuality, social class, economic status, or any other external or accidental thing about people.

Not only does Paul tell us in Romans 1:16–17 that the gospel is the power of God to save *everyone* who believes—he also says that the gospel reveals the *righteousness of God*. For many Christians this expression "the righteousness of God" is *daunting*—if not outright *frightening*. This was certainly the case for the sixteenth-century Augustinian monk, the young Martin Luther. Luther said he hated this expression—*God's righteousness*. He said it filled him with such a terrifying sense of God's holiness and moral purity, such an appalling sense of his own sin and guilt, and such an ominous dread of God's judgment and wrath that he hated this scripture as he hated no other. But then he experienced the revelation of God's righteousness in the gospel and this changed everything. He came to understand the righteousness of God as this has been revealed in Jesus Christ and it was utterly life-transforming!

As we have seen, the natural human religious instinct—and this is what got the young Martin Luther into so much bother—is our tendency to think *behaviorally* rather than *relationally*. We instinctively think of righteousness in behavioral or ethical terms. Consequently, we think that righteousness means right behavior or holiness of life. When we think of *God's* righteousness we think about *God's* behavior—God's hatred of sin and God's judgment and wrath against those who commit sin. The thought of this righteous God therefore terrifies us—a bit like it was for Peter when he first encountered Jesus. We read him saying in Luke 5:8: "Go away from me, Lord! I am a sinful man!"

Because of our tendency to think *behaviorally* rather than *relationally*, when we think about *our* righteousness we instinctively think about *our* behavior; what it is and what it ought to be—and the great chasm that separates the two. We think that our righteousness must consist in our being sinlessly holy and ethically perfect, and the thought of trying to climb this mighty moral mountain fills us with despair and convinces us that we must be hypocrites or fools to even try. Like the young Martin Luther therefore, talk of God's righteousness sows the seeds by which we secretly begin to resent God.

Now the thing about lies is that they are always more powerful when they contain a bit of truth. Consequently, the more truth a lie contains, the more powerful it becomes. It is certainly true that righteousness *does* have a behavioral aspect, but this is not its primary meaning—and understanding this changes everything. There are *three* aspects to the meaning of this profoundly important biblical concept. This is what makes righteousness such an incredibly rich and life-giving concept, but also such a multilayered and therefore prone to being misunderstood concept. This is why it is so very important, as we saw with faith in chapter 2, that we *distinguish* these three aspects while also keeping them in their *right order*.

The primary and overarching aspect of the meaning of righteousness is *relational* and *covenantal*. This means that, first and foremost, righteousness means faithfulness to a covenantal relationship. The second aspect follows from this and is *behavioral* and *ethical*. Therefore, second, righteousness means behavior that corresponds to and bears faithful witness to the primary overarching covenantal relationship from which it flows. Then, third, there is the whole question concerning who is and who isn't righteous—and who it is who makes this judgment. So the third aspect of the meaning of righteousness is *legal* and *judicial*. It concerns who has the judicial authority and competence to judge someone righteous or unrighteous—and therefore *who doesn't!*

These three aspects are brought to light in the story of David cutting off the tassel of Saul's cloak in the cave. In 1 Samuel 24:16–17 we read:

> Saul asked, "Is that your voice, David my son?" And he wept aloud. "You are more righteous than I," he said. "You have treated me well, but I have treated you badly."

The Righteousness of God—So Is This a Good Thing or a Bad Thing?

The key thing to note is that Saul and David existed within a covenantal relationship—the relationship of king to subject and subject to king—and therefore both had behavioral obligations toward one another. However, whereas David was trying to be loyal to Saul, Saul was trying to assassinate David—and so David was clearly doing a better job of being faithful to the relationship between them than Saul was. It is *this* comparative faithfulness that Saul acknowledged when he said "you are more righteous than I." Consequently, he wasn't commenting on David's holiness of life or moral purity or suggesting that he was sinlessly perfect. Rather, he was commenting on the fact that David's *behavior* bore more faithful witness to the covenantal relationship between them than his did. This story also hints at the third aspect of the meaning of righteousness concerning who has the authority to make such judgments. This is because it was the king, King Saul, who made this judgment—a judgment that is the sole prerogative of the king.

But because the gospel reveals *God's* righteousness, it reveals that the true King is not King Saul—or any other human king—it is God. What this means is that it is *God* who is the only legal judicial authority in this matter concerning who is judged righteous—and who is not. Therefore, for any human to make judgments concerning who they think is righteous or unrighteous—or even to judge *themselves* righteous or unrighteous—is to usurp the kingship of God.

It is precisely this judgment-making concerning who we regard as righteous or not that constitutes the great tragedy of our human unrighteousness. This also is what the gospel reveals; that when God mercifully judges both ourselves and others righteous—that is, to be in a right and restored relationship with God through the covenant faithfulness of Jesus Christ on our behalf—so often we are reluctant to accept God's judgment. So often (like Jonah, David, the prodigal's older brother, and the Pharisee praying in the temple) we are offended by God being merciful toward those we think undeserving of God's mercy. Our natural inclination is to appeal to what we foolishly imagine is a better authority—our own judgment—in which we typically condemn others and exonerate ourselves, or else idolise others and demonize ourselves. Moreover, we do all this judging independent of the gospel of Jesus Christ. This is why the righteousness of God revealed in the gospel begins as the revelation of God's wrath against our human unrighteousness in which we—either as Christians or as non-Christians, religious people or nonreligious—"suppress [*God's*] truth by [*our*] unrighteousness" as Paul puts it in Romans 1:18.

This is the primary meaning of righteousness—being restored to right relationship with God and, as a consequence, restored to right relationship with ourselves, with others, and with all creation through the reconciling *chesed* covenant faithfulness of God in and through Jesus Christ. So when we speak of *God's* righteousness—and especially how this is revealed in the gospel of Jesus Christ—we must understand that, first and foremost, it is Jesus Christ who is the revelation of God's righteous covenant *chesed* faithfulness. Consequently, what the gospel reveals is that at the heart and center of God's purposes from all eternity is God's determination to reconcile all humanity and all creation to himself in freedom and love through Jesus Christ in order that we might come to enjoy restored and right relationship with God, with ourselves, with our neighbors, and with all of God's good creation.

Second, flowing out of this revelation of God's covenant faithfulness in Jesus Christ—in order that we really do enjoy these relationships in authentically *relational* and *human* ways—God calls and commands us, and by his Holy Spirit enables us, to *behave* in ways that correspond and bear faithful witness to God's faithfulness toward us. Or as Paul says in Romans 1:17:

> He who through faith is righteous shall live. (NRSV)

God's commands are not arbitrary ethical rules—although any number of people have reduced them to merely this. Rather they direct us to the kind of life that aligns with and reflects the being of God—the God who *is* love. As Paul says in Galatians 5:14:

> The entire law [of God] is fulfilled in keeping this one command:
> "Love your neighbor as yourself."

Therefore the kind of life God directs us toward, and by the power of the Holy Spirit enables us toward, is the kind of life that corresponds to and aligns with the being of the God who has created both us and the world in which we live in order that we may be rightly related to God, to ourselves, to our neighbors, and to God's creation. What this means is that the life God directs us toward corresponds to and aligns with the moral fabric of the universe. And so for us to live in contradiction to God is to live in contradiction to both our internal human reality as well as the external reality of the world that God has created for us to live within.

Then third, God declares to us by his kingly authority that in and through and *because of* Jesus Christ we now possess God's judicial verdict of righteousness—that is, we are declared by the only true and competent judicial authority to be genuinely restored to right relationship with God. The reason God pronounces his judicial verdict of righteousness (God's justification) upon us is to assure us that although God does speak against our sin and does desire right behavior from us, it is not our behavior (good or bad) that is the originating or sustaining cause of our being restored to right relationship with God. Rather it is the covenantal *chesed* faithfulness and righteousness of God (God's grace) made effective for us in Jesus Christ through the enabling power of the Holy Spirit that accomplishes and sustains this new relational reality. This is where God's wrath is revealed also. God's wrath is God's holy opposition to all that suppresses the truth, knowledge, and acceptance of God's righteous decision to reconcile all creation to himself in Jesus Christ—especially whenever and wherever this truth and knowledge of *God's* righteousness is suppressed by human unrighteousness; especially whenever and wherever people remain willfully ignorant of God's righteousness and seek to establish their own.

Ever since Martin Luther, this doctrine of righteousness through faith (or justification, as it is often called) has been taught by most Protestants with two key emphases: first, our justification through faith is the answer to our search for a gracious God; and second, this forms the basis of our evangelistic endeavors. In other words, our knowing that God holds us to be guilty sinners yet mercifully forgives us on account of our faith in the atoning death of Jesus means that we are to preach *law* in order to highlight *sin* thus creating *guilt* so as to encourage *repentance* and in this way prepare people to receive God's *gracious acceptance.*

For more than twenty years I was an ardent preacher of this doctrine. However, it began to concern me that I was always going to *Paul* for my preaching texts. Almost all my sermons on the doctrine of justification or righteousness by faith—a doctrine I accepted as "gospel" (and also "the" gospel)—were drawn from Paul; in particular from key parts of Romans, Galatians, and Philippians. But gradually it began to dawn on me, then concern me—and then deeply trouble me—that there is very little in the gospels from *Jesus himself* that can be easily pressed into service to preach the doctrine of righteousness by faith in this Reformation-inspired way. Moreover, when the effort *is* made to do this, it is difficult to escape the gnawing suspicion that Jesus is being made to conform to a Martin Luther–inspired reading of Paul. It seems clear to me now that the traditional Protestant approach to the doctrine of justification is primarily concerned with a person's *individual* relationship with God and that the missional imperative of this doctrine consists in urging this *privatized* pursuit of right relationship with God upon others at the moment of their conversion.

I don't think it is wrong to use the doctrine of justification in this way because our personal relationship with God clearly has its proper place. My concern however is that if we think that this is *all* that the doctrine consists of—or that this is its *primary* purpose—the effect is to impoverish our understanding of both the gospel and the mission of God. However, when we take our Martin Luther–inspired spectacles off and simply consider the ministry of Jesus in its totality—it comes as a shock (and then as a great joy) to discover that Jesus doesn't seem to be *primarily* concerned with a person's *individual* relationship with God, or with assisting us in our search for a gracious God, or even with confronting people before the bar of God's justice by preaching law in order to highlight sin thus creating guilt so as to encourage repentance. Rather, what we see Jesus doing is announcing that in his very person God's kingdom rule has come near, inviting people to participate in this new reality in community together with him, and then going around demonstrating what the arrival of God's justice, peace, and restoration to rights looks like. Jesus does this through healing the sick, casting out demons, confronting hard-hearted religious law-obedience and hypocrisy, standing in solidarity with outcasts and the dispossessed—and gathering people together in community to bear witness to the new kingdom reality God is bringing into being.

When we read Paul in light of *this* (rather than in light of Martin Luther's privatized search for a gracious God) we see that what he is doing is actually exactly the same as Jesus is doing! In other words Paul's *primary* use of the doctrine of righteousness through faith is not to convert people through gospel proclamation or to promote their personal relationship with God, but rather to further the all-inclusive kingdom mission of God that Jesus has inaugurated in his ministry. It is important we understand that Paul's primary reason in writing Romans is not his concern that these Roman Christians find a gracious God or to confront the sin of the Gentile world—but in order to enlist the logistical support of this mixed group of Jewish and Gentile believers for his planned mission trip to the people of Spain (15:14–33).[2] The problem Paul faces, however, is that the overwhelming majority of first-century Jews and Gentiles (including the Christians in Rome) regarded the indigenous people of Spain with contempt. Consequently, Paul uses the doctrine of righteousness by faith to

---

2. Jewett, *Romans*, 1–91

demonstrate that God does not make distinctions between people on the basis of race, culture, ancestral privilege, religious law-obedience, gender, sexuality, social class, economic status, or any other external or accidental thing about them—there is no distinction between people. As he says in Romans 3:23-24:

> For all have sinned and fallen short of the glory of God and are justified freely by his grace through the redemption that came by Christ Jesus.

What this means is that these smug Jesus-believers in Rome need to get off their religious high horses and be willing to recognize that "the gospel is God's power to save all who believe—the Jew first and also the [indigenous people of Spain]." For this reason, Paul understood himself to be "under obligation to both the *civilized*" (like the Christians in Rome imagined themselves to be) "and the *ignorant*" (like they thought the indigenous people of Spain were). Therefore these Roman Christians needed to change the way they regarded both themselves as well as the people of Spain:

> Or do you show contempt for the riches of his kindness, forbearance and patience, not realizing that God's kindness is intended to lead you to repentance? (Rom 2:4)

In Galatians he uses the doctrine of justification to counter the Judaizing influence of James and Peter, who were reinstating the Old Testament food purity laws and thus excluding Gentile Christians from participating with Jewish Christians in table fellowship together (2:11–21). And in Philippians he uses it in a similar way to counter Jewish Christians who were insisting that Gentile Christians must be circumcised before they can participate in the full fellowship of God (3:1–11).

Therefore, instead of using the doctrine of righteousness through faith to serve a privatized *individualistic* purpose—a purpose that can so easily slide into a smug other-world-focused spiritual elitism—Paul uses it to serve a much larger *communal* this-world purpose. Paul's purpose is that we must understand that in light of Jesus Christ *all* people stand on the same level before God, no matter who they are. In this way the doctrine of justification through faith apart from religious law-obedience powerfully confronts all manner of ideologies that foster and fester distinctions between people—supremacist racist bigotry, nationalistic self-interest, and all forms of social injustice rooted in fear of "the other." In this way the doctrine of justification, rightly understood, is so relevant to and sorely needed in our contemporary twenty-first-century tribalistic, polarizing, fear-filled context.

11

The Salvation of God
—so what does a saved person look like?

In the Genesis creation account (1:26–27) we read:
> Then God said, "Let us make mankind in our image, in our likeness, so that they may rule over the fish in the sea and the birds in the sky, over the livestock and all the wild animals, and over all the creatures that move along the ground." So God created mankind in his own image, in the image of God he created them; male and female he created them.

Down through the centuries Christians have wondered what *part* of our human nature precisely bears God's image. Most ideas about this take aspects of our humanness that we regard as being especially impressive and then point to these as bearing God's image. But how people think about themselves in relation to God has enormous power—both for good and for ill.

Historically in Western Christendom culture one of the most influential ideas is that God's image in human beings is our *rational intelligence*—the power of our minds that gives us intellectual mastery over the world of thought and ideas. This was a key factor that drove the renaissance and the scientific revolution. Another is that God's image in humanity is our *creative ability*—the skill of our bodies that gives us technological mastery over the world of things and action. This was a key factor that drove the colonial expansion of Europe and the industrial revolution.

Clearly, human rationality and creativity are not bad things. But if we think that it is our rationality and creativity that are the decisive bearers of God's image in our humanity then this is hugely problematic. If we emphasize our rational intelligence this so easily devalues people who are not intellectually gifted. As Colin Gunton so forcefully reminds us, it so easily relegates to a lower level of humanness people with mental illnesses and disabilities. It also leads to the arrogant presumption that our human reason is uncorrupted, thus encouraging foolish overconfidence in the power of our intellects. Alternatively if we emphasize our creative ability, this so easily devalues people who are unable to make a worthwhile economic, artistic, or athletic contribution while elevating the status of those who use their creativity to become rich and powerful. Moreover, when we harness our rational intelligence and creative abilities to political and industrial power (but disconnect them from an ethical basis that would otherwise guide these powers in wholesome and humane ways) they risk becoming sources of destructive exploitation of people and the environment.[1]

One of the consequences of this kind of thinking is that it has encouraged us to suppose that because we are created in God's image and likeness we can therefore determine the being of God—*by examining ourselves!* When we ask the question "Who is God?" or "What is God truly like?" Christians have often responded by using lots of "omni" words. For example, that God is *omni*-powerful, *omni*-knowledgeable, *omni*-everywhere at the same time, and *omni*-every time at the same where. Additionally, philosophers have often described God using expressions like "Unmoved Mover," "Prime Cause," and "The Ground of All Being." But when we scratch the surface of this language it starts to look as though God is merely being described in terms of human intelligence and creativity—that "God" is simply a projection of the human ego thrown up upon the heavens.

This happens in two ways. The first is that God is described as the exact *opposite* of ourselves, for example: we are finite so God must be infinite; we are weak so God must be all-powerful; we change and decay so God must be changeless and incorruptible; we suffer and die so God must be immortal and unable to suffer. This approach makes God look like a hugely magnified negative photographic image of a *normal* human being. Alternatively, God is described as an *ideal* human raised to the *n*th degree, for example: we are rational beings so God must be super-rational and all knowing; we are creative beings so God must be the master architect and

---

1. Gunton, *Creation and the New Creation*, 106–7, 194, 208.

craftsman of the universe; we make plans for the future so God must have a grand plan for all creation worked out to the very last detail. This approach makes God look like Superman on steroids.

What these approaches do therefore is to take those aspects of our human being we least admire and make these precisely what God is *not*—or else those aspects we most admire about ourselves and make magnified versions of these the primary attributes of God. The consequence of this is to deify ourselves, which of course was really the secret agenda all along! But we should be very cautious about thinking of God and ourselves primarily as rational and creative beings, because this risks completely bypassing *relationship*. We can be rational and creative as solitary individuals without any belonging or community—but we can't be *loving*. This is the great tragedy of our Western Christendom cultural heritage—by privileging our intellects and our abilities over our relationships this has so often led to a profound sense of existential and relational loneliness, disconnection, and alienation—from ourselves, from others, and from the created environment. However, when we begin with "God *is* love," as we have done, this enables us to understand God primarily as a *relational God* and ourselves as *relational beings* created *for relationship*.

Our first relationship is with God. This is our primary relationship and the reason God has created both the world and ourselves as human beings. Jesus says:

> Love the Lord your God with all your heart and with all your soul and with all your mind. This is the first and greatest commandment. (Matt 22:37–38)

This command directs us to our primary relationship with God. It is God's intention that we should find our greatest joy and fulfillment in purposefully choosing to know God with our minds, faithfully deciding to trust God with our hearts, and joyfully seeking to honor God with our whole mind-body beings. But even if we don't have the sort of relationship with God Jesus speaks of, this doesn't mean we don't have *any sort* of relationship with God. For better or worse every one of us has some sort of a relationship with God—it is impossible for us not to! Whether we love God or reject God; whether we respond to his invitation or try to flee from his presence; whether we entrust our lives to God's motherly and fatherly care or refuse, we nevertheless have a relationship with God we cannot unmake or destroy. As God's human creatures it is impossible for us to make ourselves *God-less*. Therefore all that we are and do, one way or another—whether we are consciously aware of it or not, whether openly or secretly, knowingly or unknowingly; whether from out of our functionality or our dysfunctionality; whether witnessed by our brokenness or our wholeness—bears witness to this fundamental truth about ourselves.

Our second relationship is with ourselves. Jesus continues from the greatest commandment, saying:

> And the second commandment is like it: Love your neighbor as yourself.

As yourself! This means we have a relationship with ourselves. As relational beings made in God's image we not only have awareness of God but also awareness of self. For better or worse every one of us has some sort of a relationship with ourselves—it is impossible for us not to! Whether we loath ourselves and feel utterly worthless, or whether we feel super self-confident and strut about as narcissists, these are all expressions of our self-relationship. Flowing out of the primary relational fact that we cannot make ourselves *God-less* it is also true that we cannot make ourselves *self-less*. Therefore all that we are and do, one way or another—whether we are consciously aware of it or not, whether openly or secretly, knowingly or unknowingly; whether from out of our functionality or our dysfunctionality; whether witnessed by our brokenness or our wholeness—bears witness to this truth about ourselves also.

Our third relationship is with others. Jesus says we are to

> love your neighbor as yourself.

This commandment directs us to our relationship with other people—that we are to treat others with the same consideration we treat ourselves. When we are in our right minds we care for our needs, look to our interests, and try to make the best of our lives. Jesus says we should have the same degree of care and consideration for others as we do for ourselves. However, if we don't have *this* sort of a relationship with other people, this doesn't mean we don't have *any* sort relationship with them. For better or worse every human being has some sort of a relationship with other people—it is impossible for us not to! Whether we have a beautiful relationship with our mother or an angry relationship with our long-dead father—these are relationships with others that have an impact upon us because we cannot make ourselves *other-less*. As with our relationships with God and ourselves, our relationships with others, one way or another, all bear witness to this truth about us.

And fourth, because God has created us as *physical* beings to live upon a *physical* earth, this means that we have a relationship with the world of *physical* things. We are mind-body material beings who therefore require material things for our very survival. We have a relationship with both the things God has created and the things we make out of what God has created—it is impossible for us not to! Whether we are loving stewards of God's creation and content with little or much, or exploiters of the environment in a greed-fuelled economic lust for more, these behaviors all reflect our relationship with the world of things. Therefore, as with our other relationships, flowing out of the primary relational fact that we cannot make ourselves *God-less*, it is also true that we cannot make ourselves *world-less* or *thing-less*. Consequently all that we are and do, one way or another, whether positively or negatively, knowingly or unknowingly, bears witness to this truth about ourselves.

Although we must clearly distinguish these relationships from one another we must never separate or divide them off from one another. God has not created us to be fragmented beings whose lives can be divided up into different relational boxes that can be sealed off from each other. Rather, God has created us as whole beings to live in four fundamental relationships that are distinct yet interconnected and inseparable. We delude ourselves if we think that what we do in one relationship has no bearing on our other relationships or that what we do with our bodies has no effect on our souls. We are whole soul-body beings and what we do in one relationship impacts upon the others.

For example, if we are greedy (we have a covetous relationship with *things*); envious (we have an exploitative relationship with *others*); and addicted to pornography and junk food (we have an unrighteous relationship with our *emotional and physical selves*)—these dysfunctions will corrode the integrity of our relationship with God; weaken our relationship with our families; and undermine our spiritual, social, emotional, and physical well-being. We delude ourselves if we think that what we do in our private lives has no bearing on our public lives or what we do in our business transactions has no connection to our spiritual health. These distinctions are arbitrary human constructs. As far as God is concerned there is no such thing as a private life unrelated to a public life. We simply have our life that consists of four distinct but inseparable relationships!

One way of thinking relationally about "salvation" is to understand that what God is saving us *to* or *for* is God's peace in all its fullness in all the different relationships we sustain. The Hebrew word typically translated "peace" is *shalom*. But compared to God's *shalom*, our word "peace" is very weak. In English, peace means an absence of conflict and a state of tranquility and calm—which is good as far as it goes. But it is very often the case that human peace, like the "Peace of Rome," is a peace that is established on *someone else's* terms and to *their* advantage. However, God's *shalom* is a peace that respects the humanity, dignity, culture, resources, and aspirations of *all* people. In biblical thought, God's *shalom* is much deeper, wider, and higher than human peace. This means that God's *shalom* is a holistic conception of wellness and health that embraces the totality of who we are in all the different dimensions of our lives and across all our different relationships.

In terms of our relationship with God, God's *shalom* concerns our spiritual wellness and health. God wants us to have a healthy relationship with him and therefore is deeply concerned with our relational health and well-being so that we may enjoy both peace *with* God and the peace *of* God. Peace *with* God refers to our external objective relationship status with God that has been secured for us by Jesus Christ when one died for all. The peace *of* God is our internal subjective enjoyment of the new external objective relationship status we have with God as something that we feel, experience, and know as a reality in our lives as a result of our accepting this and being reconciled to God. When we remain alienated from and unreconciled to God we alienate ourselves from the peace *of* God—regardless of how we might feel. But when we respond to God's gracious invitation and know his love for us and therefore respond to this by seeking to know, love, and trust God in return, we enter into the true relationship status we have with God through Jesus Christ—our new relationship of peace *with* God—and in this way begin to enjoy the peace *of* God. Perhaps we do not always *feel* this peace because feelings come and go—but at a deep level our living in the peace of God is our knowing we are relationally right with God and living in the love of God in and through Jesus Christ.

In terms of our relationship with ourselves, God's *shalom* concerns our emotional, psychological, intellectual, and physical wellness and health. But we are not well people. When we consider all the unhappiness, anger, and feelings of worthlessness so many people experience—all the depression, self-loathing, and suicidal tendencies—all the alienation from self, feelings of guilt, and shame people suffer, it is clear that we are not well people. When we consider all the drug and alcohol abuse, all the medicines that are prescribed and consumed, all the illnesses and ailments that afflict people, and all the phobias and neuroses that so many suffer it is very clear that we are not well people. Irenaeus, the second-century Bishop of Lyon, once said—and I think very truly—"The glory of God is a human being *truly alive*." I am told that people who have had a profound encounter with God often report experiencing a deep sense of wellness and vitality—that their senses are heightened, their minds sharper, and they are filled with an intoxicating feeling of health and energy. Perhaps this lies at the heart of so much drug abuse and alcoholism—a kind of secular shortcut to trying to experience God's *shalom*.

In terms of our relationship with others, God's *shalom* concerns our social, relational, family, and community wellness and health. This means it embraces all the different dimensions of our lives, including the economic, political, cultural, and social. The *shalom* of God is therefore all about the health and wellness not just of people as *individuals* but as families and communities and nations across the entire globe. Consequently, God's *shalom* is concerned with economic, political, and social justice. It is concerned with acting justly and loving mercy and walking humbly with God—both as individuals and in community together. God's *shalom* is concerned that the widow and the orphan, the tax collector and outcast, and the alien and stranger are *all* included and embraced and receive adequate resources so they too may live with dignity—that they too may enjoy God's peace in ways that respect the humanity, culture, and aspirations of *all* people. God's shalom—our being *saved* in this relational sense—therefore includes engaging in the hard work of reconciliation and forgiveness toward those who have treated us unjustly and those we in turn have treated unjustly.

And in terms of our relationship with the created environment, and the things that we make out of the things God has made, God's *shalom* concerns the wellness and health of our world. God's salvation concerns how we treat our rivers and oceans, our atmosphere and soil, and our animals and plants. It therefore concerns how we use God's living creatures as economic resources. The *shalom* of God also concerns how we relate to material things—the things we desire and demand through our economic purchasing decisions which in turn determine what gets produced in factories around the world, under what conditions, at whose cost, and for whose benefit and profit. It concerns whether we are contented or greedy and whether we are generous or consumed by a never-satisfied, selfish, grasping desire for more.

Finding Love

As the prophet Isaiah describes what God's salvation *shalom* looks like, he paints a picture of contentment and justice across all our relationships—especially our relationship with God's living creatures and their relationships with each other. In 11:5-9, Isaiah says:

> God will rule his people with justice and integrity. Wolves and sheep will live together in peace, and leopards will lie down with young goats. Calves and lion cubs will feed together, and little children will take care of them. Cows and bears will eat together, and their calves and cubs will lie down in peace. Lions will eat straw as cattle do. Even a baby will not be harmed if it plays near a poisonous snake. On Zion, God's sacred hill, there will be nothing harmful or evil. The land will be as full of knowledge of the Lord as the seas are full of water.

As we continue to think relationally about God's salvation and the *shalom* he calls us to, the thing that is so compelling, and which points us to the true nature of God's salvation, is that we see all these things at work in Jesus Christ. When we ask ourselves, "What does a saved person look like?" the Bible points us to Jesus Christ. And when we look at Jesus what we see is someone who is fully integrated, fully authentic, and fully faithful in *all* his relationships. In Luke 2:52 we read that

> Jesus grew in wisdom and stature, and in favor with God and man.

Here we see the intellectual, physical, spiritual, and social dimensions of Jesus' life holding together—fully integrated, fully authentic, and fully faithful. His inner life, his outward life, his vertical relationship with God, and his horizontal relationships with his neighbors are held together with integrity and in harmony. In Jesus there is no artificial separation between his private life and his public life and no divergence between his physical life and his spiritual life. Rather, what we see is *one* life—one life fully integrated and fully authentic, lived with integrity and faithfulness across *all* his relationships.

I am convinced that it is in his life of holistic relational integrity that we see both the true humanity of Jesus and what a fully saved person looks like—and therefore we see the true salvation that God is calling us to. Moreover, it is in his relational integrity that we see the true sinlessness and virtue of Jesus—and thus the true life in all its abundance and *shalom* God is calling us to participate in. However, because Christians have had a historical tendency to think of key biblical categories primarily in *behavioral* rather than *relational* terms, we have tended to think of sinlessness and virtue primarily in terms of bad behavior we don't do and good behavior we *do* do, rather than in terms of integrity and faithfulness in our relationships.

We saw these two different ways of thinking in the prayer of the two men in the temple in Luke 18:14 we looked at in the previous chapter:

> I tell you that this man, rather than the other, went home justified [or in the right] before God.

"Justified" or "in the right before God" is what many Christians would understand as "being saved." But notice that, like King Saul's statement to David, this is not a description concerning the tax collector's virtuous *behavioral actions*, but rather it is a description of his *relationship status*. So often we have tended to think, like the Pharisee, that to be "righteous before God" means we must focus on doing virtuous behavioral actions and avoid doing bad ones, rather than living with integrity and faithfulness in all our relationships. As a result, Christians have tended to focus energy on living a *pious* life.

Now "pious" is not a bad word—it means living a life of deep religious devotion marked by acts of holiness and virtue. But in popular culture, "pious" or "piety" nowadays has a very negative connotation. It refers to someone who is so focused on their own inner goodness that they come across as morally smug and judgmental and in this way they alienate themselves from genuine relationship with others. They come across like the Pharisee in the parable—totally preoccupied with evaluating the moral worth of their own lives and, as a consequence, so prone to condemning the moral failures of others, as well as holding themselves aloof from them in order to avoid being contaminated by them. Our behavior does of course matter because the character of our behavior bears witness to the quality of our relationships, but the practice of Christian *piety* shouldn't be our primary focus. Our primary focus should be living with integrity and faithfulness in all our relationships as this is modeled for us by Jesus.

The Pharisee in the parable provides an excellent example of someone who makes *behavior* the primary lens through which he understands the life of faith. But the problem with this is that it risks undermining our *relationships*, and in this way rendering them inauthentic. We end up thinking we have to try and please God by doing spiritually impressive things instead of simply trusting God and delighting in the fact that we have a restored relationship with God, with ourselves, with others, and with all creation through faith in Jesus Christ. Thinking about salvation primarily in terms of pious behavior risks our relationship with God becoming inauthentic. We risk becoming anxious that God will find fault with our behavior and turn away from us and so we risk hiding our true selves from God instead of openly confessing the truth about ourselves to God in the sure knowledge that we are *already* and therefore *always* surrounded by God's eternal loving-kindness.

We also risk ending up having an inauthentic relationship with ourselves. Instead of living in grace and truth with ourselves we risk becoming emotionally dishonest as we pretend to be someone else—a fake person we think might be better than our real self that God and others will be more impressed by. As a result, our true self becomes hidden from ourselves. Furthermore, we risk ending up having an inauthentic relationship with others. Instead of our behavior toward other people arising out of a genuine relationship of mutual regard, care, and consideration, we risk using our practice of Christian piety as a kind of religious technique to try and impress them or manipulate them so that we can feel good about ourselves. The upshot of having an inauthentic relationship with God, self, and others is that we inevitably fall back on our fourth primary relationship—our relationship with the world of things—in order to find the fulfillment that inevitably eludes our grasp. But in doing so we contaminate and pollute this relationship as well because, as Jesus says in Luke 12:15, a person's life doesn't consist in the abundance of their possessions.

But we see none of this inauthenticity in Jesus! We see nothing of the practice of some abstract concept of Christian piety that risks alienating him from God, his true self, other people, and the world. Instead what we see is that all his relationships hold together—fully integrated, fully authentic, and fully faithful. The true sinlessness, true piety, and true holiness of Jesus is found in his relational wholeness, faithfulness, and integrity. The true holiness of Jesus is found in the fact that he loves God with all his heart and mind and soul and strength, and that he loves his neighbor as himself. The true virtue of Jesus is found in his complete confidence in God to meet his every need and so he is fully at peace. The true goodness of Jesus is found in the fact that he never seeks to justify himself in the eyes of others, for in every way he knows he is loved by God and accepted by God. And the true piety of Jesus is found in the fact that he does not secretly try to cover his shame or hide his true self from the gaze of others, for he has no shame to cover and his true self is open for all to see. The true moral purity of Jesus is found in the fact that he completely trusts in God as his loving Lord and so he never abuses love and lordship in his relationships with people or things. In Jesus we see love and lordship holding together in perfect grace and truth. In Jesus love never degenerates into lust or greed, and lordship never degenerates into the domination and exploitation of others. The true righteousness of Jesus is found in the fact that he is supremely secure, supremely free, supremely alive, and supremely at peace with himself—for his security, freedom, life, and identity are supremely grounded in God.

Consequently what we definitely *don't* see in Jesus is an insecure, pompous religious pretender who is always trying to validate himself; someone who is so focused on proving his own inner goodness that he comes across like the Pharisee in the temple; someone who seeks to separate himself from others he deems less worthy or less deserving of God's favor. But what we *do* see in Jesus is someone who is genuinely authentic and faithful in all his relationships, and therefore someone who is genuinely human as God intends humans to be—or as Irenaeus would say, "a human being fully alive."

One of the consequences of thinking relationally about God's salvation is that it challenges us to reexamine much of what has been typically regarded as the practice of Christian holiness—much of which owes far more to passages like Psalm 15 and the Pharisee praying in the temple than it does to Jesus. When we consider the life of Jesus we see nothing of the kind of abstract religious moral purity practiced by the Pharisees—and by many pious Christians throughout history who have incarnated lives that seek separation from those "others" or "the world" who they fear will defile them. Instead, what we see in Jesus is the active pursuit of God's reconciling *chesed* faithfulness among others that seeks God's saving *shalom* for all people, no matter who. What we see in Jesus therefore is not *separation from* people, but *engagement with* people. Moreover, at no point do we see Jesus being anxious that this engagement will defile his holiness or threaten his relationship with God. What this all means is that it is this life of authentic faithfulness in all his relationships we see in Jesus that is the "template," as it were, concerning God's plan as to what *our* humanity genuinely consists of—and in the saving purposes of God shall indeed be. In other words, it is in Jesus Christ that we see what a saved person actually looks like!

When we see this true humanity in Jesus we recognize it as something that we long for in ourselves. There is something within us that recognizes in *Jesus* what *we* were made for and long to be ourselves. In the fragmented pieces of our own humanity and in our broken attempts to establish our own righteousness we catch a glimpse and reflection of the wholeness, relational integrity, and true humanity that we see in Jesus. As we gaze on the true humanity of Jesus it fills us with a kind of *homesickness* and longing for something that we know should be ours also—something we instinctively know we were made for, but which has slipped from our grasp—our *true home* that we recognize as ours, but don't know how to get back there. As we gaze upon the true humanity of Jesus what we see is a truly saved person—and therefore what, by God's grace and transforming power, we also shall be.

But we must look deeper than this and we can only look deeper by faith. This is because Jesus is not only the *template* of our true humanity and righteousness—and therefore the picture of our true salvation—he is also the *promise* that God is already at work restoring our true humanity to us. Jesus is God's assurance to us that God is in the business of saving us to his *shalom*! Moreover what we must understand is that God's work of restoration of our true humanity and relational wholeness—that is, our salvation—takes place in three moments.

The first salvation moment is in Jesus Christ. The Apostle Paul says in 2 Corinthians 5:17:

> Therefore, if anyone is in Christ, the new creation has come: The old has gone, the new is here!

This means that when God, in and as Jesus Christ, became fully human and as our representative "one for all" died and was raised for all (and therefore *all* died and were raised in him), in this utterly unique event of God's *chesed* faithfulness, God's new creation came into being. In Jesus Christ, God has made this new creation an objective reality that has changed the status and situation of all humanity and all creation. Consequently, this is something we are able to speak of as an accomplished reality using the past tense—something that God *has done*—something we give profound heartfelt thanks for in the present.

The second salvation moment is through the Holy Spirit. Again in 2 Corinthians (3:17–18) Paul says:

> Now the Lord is the Spirit, and where the Spirit of the Lord is, there is freedom. And we all, who with unveiled faces contemplate the Lord's glory, are being transformed into his image with ever-increasing glory, which comes from the Lord, who is the Spirit.

The Salvation of God—So What Does a Saved Person Look Like?

The reality of God's new creation in Jesus is something God works into our lives as individuals, as a subjective experiential reality in a gradual process through time. God does not transform us instantaneously. God wants our relational wholeness to be genuine, and genuine relational wholeness takes time as we engage with God, with ourselves, with others, and with the world with integrity. It is by the power of the Spirit that God transforms us progressively with "ever-increasing glory." This is something therefore we must speak of as an ongoing process of "being transformed" using the present tense—something that God *is doing*—something we faithfully participate in with God in the present.

We must especially emphasize that this ongoing process of being transformed that sits at the heart of our salvation is inevitably a *painful* process. Our being saved by God through faith in Jesus does not allow us to miraculously bypass the hard and painful relational work of being reconciled to others in love—of hearing and confessing the truth concerning those who have hurt and violated us; and of hearing and confessing the truth concerning those we have hurt and violated. God saving the wicked by grace (and this includes us all) is not them (or us) getting off "scot free." God's salvation therefore does not allow us to miraculously by-pass the consequences of what we have done and become. Our being saved by God through faith in Jesus means, by the enabling power of God's Holy Spirit, our being willing to honestly and humbly face up to the truth of all these things and being willing to engage in the hard spiritual, emotional, and relational work (to the very best of our human ability) of putting right those things that have gone wrong across all the different relationships we sustain. Our being saved by God through faith in Jesus therefore is our hearing and accepting Jesus' word of welcoming of non-condemnation and, with his help, being willing to engage in the hard work of moral regeneration that flows from this:

> Neither do I condemn you, go now and leave your life of sin. (John 8:11)

And the third salvation moment is by God. In Colossians 3:4 Paul says:

> For you died, and your life is now hidden with Christ in God. When Christ, who is your life, appears, then you also will appear with him in glory.

In our baptism we accept inwardly and proclaim outwardly to others that in Jesus Christ (because one died for all and therefore all died) we personally have also died and our true life is hidden with Christ in God. However, we accept this by *faith* because we don't yet *see* this in all its glorious fullness! The final moment in which our true humanity will be restored to us in all its visible fullness and glory is when the kingdom of God fully breaks in at the return of Jesus and is the moment the true me and the true you will also appear and be with God in glory. This is our Christian salvation resurrection hope—the hope that sustains us in the present. This is something we can only speak of as an anticipated hope using the future tense—something that God *will do*; something in the present we eagerly long for.

Finding Love

God, who is the source of our being and the goal of our existence, is love. This means that we have been created *in* love, *by* love, and *for* love, and this constitutes the whole purpose of our being—to be awakened to the fact that we are already enfolded in God's eternal loving-kindness and to be consciously and experientially incorporated into this love. Although this knowledge is often obscure to us, all that we are and do bears witness to this God-created purpose for our human being. This means that our deepest human need and longing, and thus what constitutes our fundamental humanity, is being loved and loving in return—being accepted, valued, and affirmed. Conversely, our deepest human fear—and thus the greatest threat to our being truly human—is to exist in a state of lovelessness and thus believing ourselves to be alienated, rejected, and valueless. Therefore—given both our knowledge and ignorance, our wholeness and brokenness, whether openly or secretly, with conscious awareness or merely by instinct—at any given moment we are doing the best we know to secure this love or else to guard ourselves against the hurts of failed love. So regardless of how our behavior manifests itself on the surface, the great inner driver behind all that we are and do is our quest to secure acceptance, value, and affirmation; and to avoid alienation, rejection, and shame. It is in seeking these positives and avoiding these negatives in ways that miss the purpose of God that lies at the root of all our anxieties, dysfunctions, and miseries.

However, the tragic irony is that if our goal is to try and *find* love—God's or anyone else's—then we will inevitably live in fearful insecurity. This is because our minds will forever turn to our adequacy—whether we are attractive enough or good enough to win or merit the love of another. And if we do succeed then our anxiety turns to how we may maintain what we have gained. The Bible tells us "God is love" (1 John 4:16). Unfortunately this has often been understood in ways that reinforce our fears. This is because it has often had its sharp radical edge blunted by treating it as "God is *loving*," thus reducing love to a mere attribute of God—something God *does* rather than *is*. Additionally, it has often been understood as a love we exist outside of and therefore our great task is to somehow find our way into it, or else exist without it.

But "God is love" is not simply describing some attribute of God. Rather, it is describing God's intrinsic being and essential nature—the very Godness of what and who God is! This means that the thing that sits at the very origin and center of the universe is love, and that our intrinsic human being and essential nature originates from out of this love. It means that we have been created *in* love, *by* love, and *for* love; and that this constitutes the whole purpose of our being—to be consciously and experientially incorporated into this love. Consequently, our human desire for love is not simply something peculiar about us that has nothing in external reality to correspond to. Rather it is something that is in us because it has been hardwired into the very fabric of our beings by the God who is love in order that we may find its fulfillment in relationship with God.

Another tragic irony in this however is that when Christians have tried to communicate these things they have often given the impression (because many believe it to be true) that in our natural condition we exist outside of God's love—that God has erected a barrier against us. And therefore the good news of Jesus is misunderstood to be about how God has opened a door through this barrier to allow certain individuals who profess faith to come through and then bolts the door shut again against everyone else who doesn't!

The nearest analogy we have to this is the relationship we have with our children. Our children don't come into the world behind a bolted door we have erected that separates them from our love. Nor is their great task to find and win our love by making themselves attractive or good enough for us to open our door to them. Rather they come into the world already surrounded by our love and their great task (and ours also) is that as they grow and develop they become aware of, learn to trust as true, and enter into the love that already surrounds them in real and genuinely relational ways. So it is with God.

The good news of Jesus Christ is that God has obliterated and destroyed all barriers and bolted doors against relationship with God. Any barriers that remain are ones that we have erected from our side. But from God's side, God wants us to know that we are already enfolded within God's eternal loving-kindness—and that this is true whether we know and accept it or not. And so what this means is that our great task is not to try and find love, but *to awaken to the reality that love has already found us.*

Bibliography

Barth, Karl. *Church Dogmatics*. Vol. II/2, *The Doctrine of God*. Translated by G. W. Bromiley et al. Edinburgh: T. & T. Clark, 1957.
———. *Church Dogmatics*. Vol. III/2, *The Doctrine of Creation*. Translated by Harold Knight et al. Edinburgh: T. & T. Clark, 1960.
———. *Church Dogmatics*. Vol. IV/1, *The Doctrine of Reconciliation*. Translated by G. W. Bromiley. Edinburgh: T. & T. Clark, 1956.
Gunton, Colin E. "Creation and the New Creation: In the Image and Likeness of God." In *The Triune Creator*, 193–211. Edinburgh: Edinburgh University Press, 1998.
Hart, David Bentley. *That All Shall Be Saved: Heaven, Hell & Universal Salvation*. New Haven: Yale University Press, 2019.
Jewett, Robert. *Romans: A Commentary*. Minneapolis: Fortress Press, 2006.
The Jewish Study Bible. Edited by Adele Berlin and Marc Zvi Brettler. Oxford: Oxford University Press, 2004.
Lewis, C. S. *The Chronicles of Narnia*. New York: HarperCollins, 2001.
McLaren, Brian. *A New Kind of Christianity: The Questions That Are Transforming the Faith*. New York: HarperOne, 2010.
Parry, Robin A., and Christopher H. Partridge. *Universal Salvation? The Current Debate*. Grand Rapids: Eerdmans, 2003.
Rohr, Richard. *Falling Upward: A Spirituality for the Two Halves of Life*. San Francisco: Jossey-Bass, 2011.
Torrance, James B. *Worship, Community & the Triune God of Grace*. Downers Grove: InterVarsity, 1996.
Voyle, Rob. "An Appreciative Inquiry Paradigm for Transitional Ministry." In *Transitional Ministry Today, Successful Strategies for Churches and Pastors*, edited by Norman B. Bendroth, 122–45. Lanham, MD: Rowman and Littlefield, 2015.

www.ingramcontent.com/pod-product-compliance
Lightning Source LLC
Chambersburg PA
CBHW072154160426
43197CB00012B/2385